FRENCH ACCENTS

FRENCH ACCENTS

AT HOME WITH PARISIAN OBJECTS AND DETAILS

ERIN SWIFT

WITH BRENNA McLOUGHLIN | PHOTOGRAPHS BY JONNY VALIANT

CLARKSON POTTER/PUBLISHERS

NEW YORK

Copyright © 2013 by Erin Swift
Photographs copyright © 2013 by Jonny Valiant

All rights reserved.
Published in the United States by Clarkson Potter/
Publishers, an imprint of the Crown Publishing Group,
a division of Random House, Inc., New York.
www.crownpublishing.com
www.clarksonpotter.com

CLARKSON POTTER is a trademark and POTTER with
colophon is a registered trademark of Random House, Inc.

Library of Congress Cataloging-in-Publication Data
Swift, Erin.
French accents/Erin Swift.
    p.   cm
Includes index.
1. Interior decoration—themes, motives. 2. Decoration
and ornament—France—themes, motives. I. Title.
NK2110.S95   2013
747—dc23 2012017639

ISBN 978-0-307-98530-9

Printed in China

Book and jacket design by Stephanie Huntwork
Jacket photography by Jonny Valiant

10 9 8 7 6 5 4 3 2 1

First Edition

TO J.R.W.

CONTENTS

INTRODUCTION

French Accents began as an exploration of the age-old questions: What is French style and how can one achieve this seemingly effortless but impeccably chic look at home? To find the answer, I traveled throughout France and the United States to photograph interiors that seemed to capture the essence of the French sensibility. No matter how different these homes were from one another, a fresh, elegant, and daring aesthetic was a common thread.

But this shared sensibility remained difficult to sum up and put into words. The details of these homes offered insight: I found consistent ideas that would make the elusive French style accessible and attainable for those born without innate savoir faire.

French Accents provides a close look at stylish homes with an eye to color, art and furnishings, objects and accents, structure, and texture. The elements of each room and scene are broken down to simplify the ideas behind them. Conversations with several homeowners allow us to learn more about their favorite rooms, their most loved shops, and their sources of inspiration. Collections of images show the abundance of choices in flooring, doorknobs, fabrics, and other details, so that you can choose what resonates with you and create your own mix of elements the way the French do.

My hope is that in reading *French Accents*, and examining the details of these homes, you will gain the dashing confidence of style seen throughout the book. You will feel empowered to layer old and new pieces, bold and muted colors, simple and rich textures, and to find your own unique way to form a look that is perfectly imperfect. In the end, I hope that you'll come away with your own definition of French style and an appreciation of details and objects that will help you make your own home indescribably beautiful.

—ERIN SWIFT

COLOR
LA COULEUR

Color is perhaps the first thing that catches the eye in homes decorated in the French style. The use and application of tone and hue in interiors vary widely, and the diversity is thrilling. But it's what these unique homes have in common that leaves the most lasting impression: they share a daring, no-rules approach to color—in furnishings, on walls and floors—that makes each space look fresh and elegantly surprising.

Some homes in the following pages use vivid shades with brio: one boasts both an emerald-green library and a magenta foyer, while in another, a ruby-red room leads right into a cornflower-blue one. On the opposite end of the spectrum are homes with walls that are all white yet, with a clever array of furnishings, manage to look just as rich and inviting as the Technicolor interiors. An all-white or solid-colored room may use one shade for the ceiling, molding, and trim, inviting the eye to take in the space as a whole, as opposed to breaking it down into its component parts. Neutrals are defined broadly to include pale blues and greys, and are inevitably accented with a pop of vibrant color. Monochromatic schemes get a twist, too, as the owners and designers employ shades ever so slightly lighter and darker than the color the room is built around—proof that even a style that appears simple is actually quite thoughtful and complex.

PRECEDING SPREAD Color and design come together in a striking door with a black wrought-iron quatrefoil grid and geometric panels. The emerald-green paint is beautiful both intact and where it has chipped away, revealing the pale wood beneath.

ABOVE An eighteenth-century settee upholstered in grey cashmere sits beneath windows with original hardware, flanked by bold black-and-white striped silk curtains; the sunlight flooding through the windows makes the dark colors look even richer.

OPPOSITE This dining room's restrained color scheme is brashly punctuated by the Verner Panton rug beneath the Christophe Delcourt table.

Be bold. Use something like Yves Klein blue against terra-cotta-colored tiles and classic French antiques. Orange and blue are complementary hues on the color wheel, which is why this look is so appealing.

ABOVE The rich neutral shades of a tan-and-chrome Le Corbusier chair and a large plaster-and-marble console are balanced by a pair of Regency-style chairs upholstered in turquoise leather.

BELOW The modified lancet arch of the window is a reference to Gothic architecture; the pink hue of the walls makes it look fresh.

OPPOSITE The kitchen combines bold Allmilmo cabinetry in cobalt with chrome details, white marble counters and backsplash, and earth-toned quarry-tile floors. The Italian kitchen table and Louis XV caned chairs, both from the eighteenth century, introduce unexpected shades, including deep green and ochre.

PREVIOUS SPREAD, LEFT This kitchen looks serene in warm neutrals and sage-green walls adorned with framed botanical prints.

PREVIOUS SPREAD, RIGHT In the sitting room, the deep colors of the walls and furnishings and the light shades in the Moroccan rug and the Kara Walker print above the fireplace create a chiaroscuro effect. Often, people try to avoid dark hues in small spaces, but in reality, saturated tones give the impression of greater dimensions.

CHAMELEON COLOR

MANY PEOPLE have had the unfortunate experience of realizing too late—maybe after the first coat of paint is dry, maybe after the second—that the color they chose for their walls isn't quite right. One explanation for this is metamerism, a phenomenon by which light changes the appearance of color. Avoid an unpleasant surprise by living with your top three or four hues before making a decision:

- Get samples of the shades you like best (no need to buy whole cans) and paint swatches of each color on your wall. Consider putting swatches on more than one wall within the room to see how the tones look from different angles.

- Over the course of a day or two, make note of how artificial light and direct and indirect sunlight affect the look of the paints.

- Pay special attention to the light on the swatches during the hours of the day you're most likely to use the room. In the bedroom, see how you like the colors at night with the lights on; view the kitchen hues in the morning and evening, and the living room options from dusk to night.

In a play on light and dark colors, the deep-purple walls and deep-red mantelpiece are juxtaposed with white and ivory in the Louis XIV–style chair covered in Lelièvre fabric and the lamp shade. A black-and-gold antique mirror frame is used to hang favorite images and other inspirations for one-of-a-kind wall art.

OPPOSITE The deep-purple bedroom features a 1940s Louis XV–style bed frame, covered in Jim Thompson fabric, with a canopy in shades of tan and purple. The 1900s Italian bedside table, Laura Ashley brass lamp, and 1880s French candlelight fixtures echo the gilded trim on the bed.

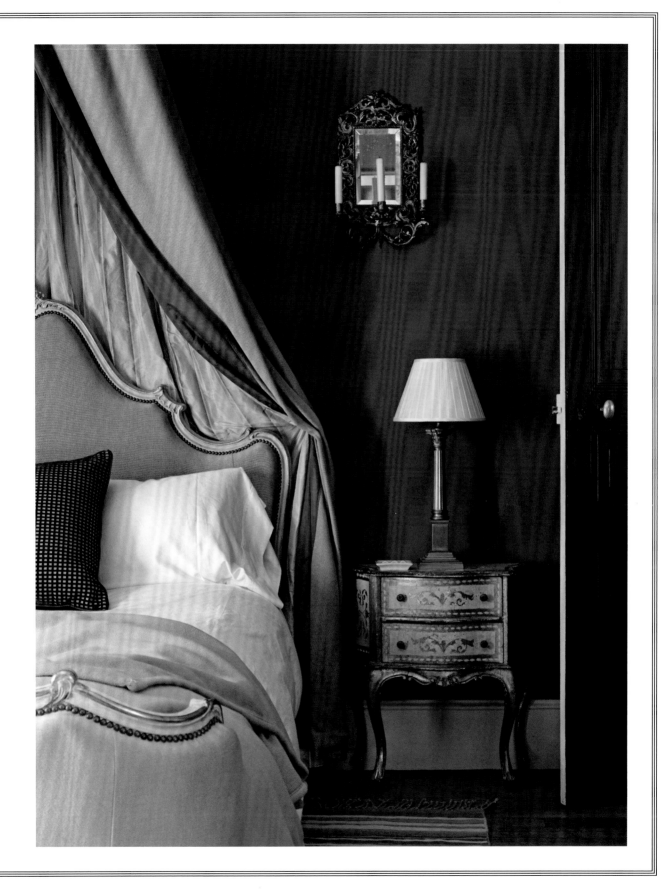

The cool grey and beige shades in this living room illustrate just how boldly sophisticated muted tones can look. A thoughtfully placed hot-pink book on an ottoman and deep-red flowers on a mahogany-and-marble Empire table add small—but powerful—doses of vividness; brass accessories add luster to the mantelpiece.

RAINBOW IN THE ROUND

TO PRIME your eye and find inspiration for the kinds of daringly stylish color schemes seen in French decorating, look to that mainstay of design, the color wheel. It was created as an arrangement of the colors present in white light, known as the spectrum, to display the relationships between them. This color wheel shows the three primary colors (blue, red, and yellow) plus the three secondary colors (green, violet, and orange), which are created when two primary colors are combined. The next extension of the color wheel includes the six tertiary colors, which are created when a primary color and its adjacent secondary color are combined, yielding red-orange, blue-violet, and yellow-green. There are endless variations of the twelve colors on the color wheel; here are a few terms that help describe them:

HUE a gradation of color that differentiates one from another (i.e., yellow-green, green, blue-green)

TINT a variation of a color created by adding white (i.e., light blue)

SHADE a variation of a color created by adding black (i.e., dark green)

TONE also referred to as value; the relative lightness or darkness of a hue

SATURATION the purity of a color

Many interesting combinations can be discovered by studying the color wheel. Start with one hue, and then look at those that occur at different angles to it on the wheel. Those angles will present color schemes with varying degrees of harmoniousness and contrast. The more distinct the hues, the more disparity there will be in the color scheme. Balance the intensity of the look by experimenting with the saturation and tone of your chosen colors, or by establishing a dominant hue and using the others as accents.

COMPLEMENTARY this refers to a pair of colors that appear opposite each other on the color wheel, such as blue and orange, or purple and yellow. A split complementary combines one color with the two colors to the right and left of its complement on the color wheel; for example, green, orange, and purple.

TRIADIC three equidistant hues combine to form a triadic color scheme.

TETRADIC four colors found at right angles to each other. These can be identified by imagining a square or rectangle imposed on a color wheel, such as red, orange, blue, and green.

ANALOGOUS a combination of hues adjacent to each other on the color wheel that together create a harmonious look; for example, blue and purple.

MONOCHROMATIC by strict definition, a monochromatic color scheme uses one color with tints, shades, and tones of that color. More broadly, a monochromatic color scheme may include one color used in combination with other hues based in that color.

Surprising presentation, for example, a shocking orange wall, highlights the uniqueness of these objects: a cast-resin bust by Oly and a brass hand-shaped bottle opener.

OPPOSITE Boldly painted walls bring out the vibrant colors of Roy Lichtenstein's *Masterpiece* and Hans Hofmann's *Cathedral*, as well as those in the twentieth-century Austrian rug. The dining table and chairs, in dark wood and cream-colored upholstery, allow this room's artwork to get its due attention.

Embrace primary colors. In a room with impressive architecture and incredible artwork, colors from the crayon box can look very grown-up. Give a serious room a makeover with easily changeable slipcovers, which are also great to use as added protection for your furnishings.

This living room offers a study in contrasts. The white-on-white walls with their intricate moldings and the neutral colors surrounding the mantel and floors receive a surprising splash of color in the form of the bright Caravane sofa and slipper chairs. The upholstered pieces are actually grey; the homeowner wanted a fresh, summery look, so she had yellow and green slipcovers made for the season. A rough-hewn antique African stool and a sleek black marble table by Italian designer Gae Aulenti offset the plushness of the sofa and chairs. Nestled among the coffee table's books and periodicals are a nude sculpture by Olivier Debré and a vivid red lobster dish.

The neutral colors of the bedroom
create a soothing atmosphere,
punctuated with vibrant orange
shams, iconic Tizio lamps, Christian
Liaigre bedside tables, plus artwork
by Marc Hispard and Ruben Alterio.

If you're not a color person, think of
using black and white as your base palette
but sneak in a pop of color. In a bedroom,
use a white duvet as a calm constant; bring
in color with sheets, shams, and coverlets,
which you can change over the years
or seasons.

Don't be afraid to make a statement in the bath; it is likely among the smallest and most private rooms in a home, so it's a great place to take a risk.

ABOVE The tub from Jacob Delafon was custom painted to become the visual centerpiece of the bathroom; its shade of blue is replicated on the walls. The 1870s bookcase, used as a linen closet, is painted in a rich ivory color, which adds a warm tone to the room.

BELOW RIGHT In this bedroom, a chic combination of muted shades brings into focus antiques and other items from the homeowner's collection, including a Chinese lacquer chest of drawers, a zinc fleur-de-lis lamp, framed artworks, and an 1890 French stool upholstered in mint-green damask. The soft and casual linens, a variation on a classic French toile, show off effortless style.

OPPOSITE Graphic art and textiles in vivid shades give the bedroom a playful look. Vintage-style posters of ski resorts and Massimo Vitali's Rosignano 2004 beach scene hint at the homeowner's favorite holiday destinations. The colors in the draperies and decorative pillows are just as cheerful.

Establish your ideal
palette for a space, and
go crazy with pattern
and art. If you use your
palette as a unifying
scheme, it doesn't matter
how many patterns or
textures you mix.

CITY OF LIGHT

THERE IS SOMETHING about the light in Paris. Though the city is known for its glow after dusk, its daytime illumination is just as noteworthy. Paris's northerly location relative to the equator situates it farther from the sun than most of the continental United States, and therefore the sunlight in Paris, even during the gloriously long days of summer, appears less intense. The city's temperate, if a little rainy, climate also affects the appearance of natural light.

These geographic factors are magnified by the many limestone buildings in Paris. The light from the faraway sun, filtered through the moisture in the air and reflected off of the famous creamy grey limestone, is rendered a bit cool, with a greyish hue. It's a moody light that gives the city a sensuous, mysterious look. And of course, as it passes through windows and into homes, it becomes the lens through which all interior design must be viewed, and it bestows these homes with that famous, sought-after je ne sais quoi. Short of moving to Paris, let its light inspire your decor by embracing variations in hue—all the colors of the rainbow can be toned down to create a moodier, cooler version that can bring a bit of Paris into your home.

The moderate climate of Paris gives the city its lush green gardens and lawns, the colors of which look all the brighter on a cloudy day, and especially beside the iron lattice of the Eiffel Tower. Bring fresh plants and flowers indoors to add color and life to your interiors.

OPPOSITE This office strikes the perfect balance between utility and style. The modern chrome-legged chair and Le Corbusier desk, plus the sleek black file cabinet from Dupré Octante, are softened by the neutral rug, artwork by Marc Hispard and Ruben Alterio on the walls, and a leather sofa topped with a fur throw.

Keep a neutral color scheme as interesting as a room full of vivid hues by mixing soft and coarse textures and angular and curved forms.

The simplicity of the white-and-black color scheme allows the room's exquisite details to shine. The monochromatic wall and ceiling are covered in neoclassical-style moldings. The furnishings are high-design pieces: Barcelona stools by Mies van der Rohe and Christian Liaigre coffee table and chairs, with Biedermeier side chairs flanking the mantel.

MOODY HUES

THE COLOR SCHEMES in French homes are appealing not only for the way they look but also for the mood they create. Color has a powerful impact on energy. Before choosing the hues of a room, first consider how you plan to use the room and how you'd like it to feel: Would you like it to be a place that encourages activity, or a peaceful environment that encourages rest and relaxation? For some rooms, the choice is clear; a bedroom should be soothing, to promote sleep. In the case of a space such as a dining room, the choice is more subjective; do you prefer to eat in a serene setting, or would you rather foster lively conversation and debate over dinner?

When you know what sort of mood you'd like to give the room, seek out tones or shades of the color that fit both the look and feel you'd like to achieve:

RED is exciting and stimulating. It is the color of passion and love.

YELLOW makes people feel optimistic and cheerful, and is believed to promote concentration.

GREEN evokes new growth as in nature, and is also associated with good health and luck.

BLUE is a calming color, due to its association with water. Because it is believed to ease the mind, heart rate, and breathing, blue encourages contemplation and creativity.

PURPLE is also considered soothing, and is associated with royalty, but also with arrogance.

BLACK suggests power, sexuality, and sophistication.

WHITE reflects sunlight and makes people feel cheerful; it also conjures notions of purity, cleanliness, and precision.

BROWN is reminiscent of earth, and so suggests comfort and endurance.

Contrast also impacts energy; as one increases, so does the other. Monochromatic and analogous color schemes have a harmonious effect, and thus make for a relatively subdued room, depending on the dominant color. High-contrast complementary color schemes excite the mind as much as they do the eye. Energy further increases with the introduction of additional colors, as in a triadic or tetradic scheme.

BRILLIANT BOLDS AND NEUTRALS

One of the easiest ways to update your color scheme, whether you want a subtle change or a dramatic one, is with paint. Not only are there endless shades to choose from, but there are also a variety of finishes, from matte to high gloss, that can completely transform a room. When discussing and describing colors at the paint store or with a decorator as you're planning your interiors, use foods and natural elements as references to give an accurate description of what you envision—chocolate and espresso are much more evocative than the word *brown*. Here are some favorite shades, inspired by the homes in the book.

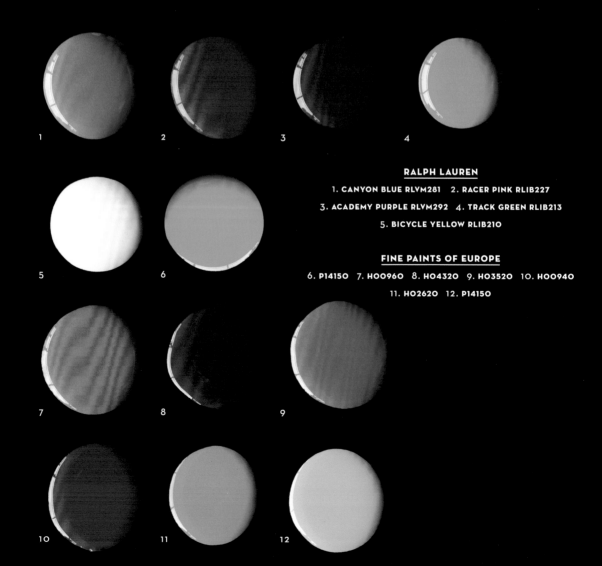

RALPH LAUREN

1. CANYON BLUE RLVM281   2. RACER PINK RLIB227
3. ACADEMY PURPLE RLVM292   4. TRACK GREEN RLIB213
5. BICYCLE YELLOW RLIB210

FINE PAINTS OF EUROPE

6. P14150   7. HO0960   8. HO4320   9. HO3520   10. HO0940
11. HO2620   12. P14150

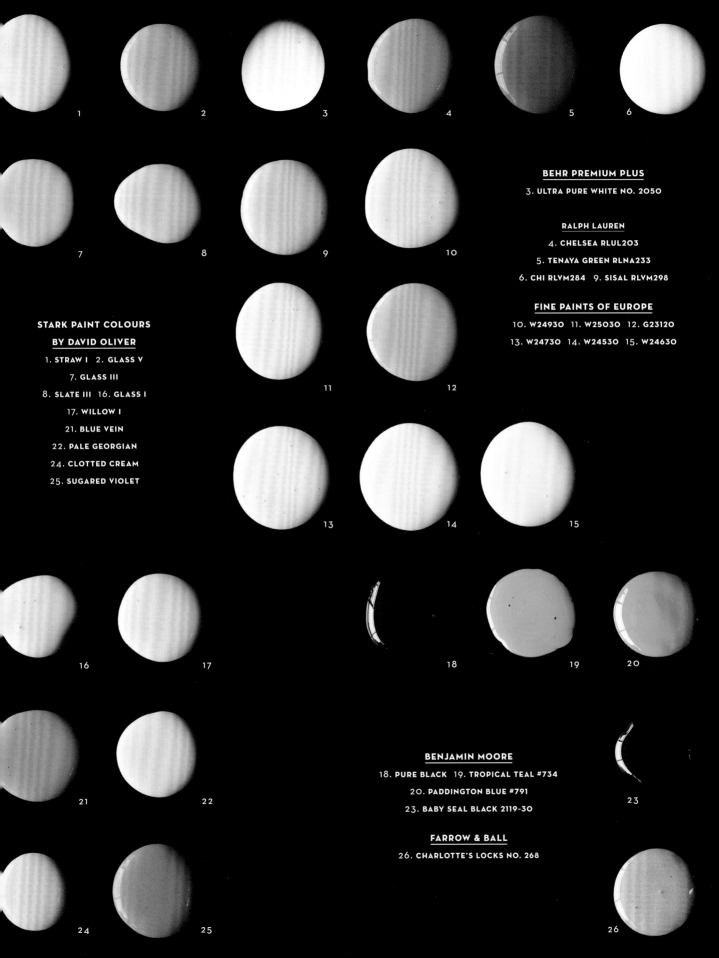

BEHR PREMIUM PLUS
3. ULTRA PURE WHITE NO. 2050

RALPH LAUREN
4. CHELSEA RLUL203
5. TENAYA GREEN RLNA233
6. CHI RLVM284   9. SISAL RLVM298

FINE PAINTS OF EUROPE
10. W24930   11. W25030   12. G23120
13. W24730   14. W24530   15. W24630

**STARK PAINT COLOURS
BY DAVID OLIVER**
1. STRAW I   2. GLASS V
7. GLASS III
8. SLATE III   16. GLASS I
17. WILLOW I
21. BLUE VEIN
22. PALE GEORGIAN
24. CLOTTED CREAM
25. SUGARED VIOLET

BENJAMIN MOORE
18. PURE BLACK   19. TROPICAL TEAL #734
20. PADDINGTON BLUE #791
23. BABY SEAL BLACK 2119-30

FARROW & BALL
26. CHARLOTTE'S LOCKS NO. 268

VINCENT FREY AND BIANCA LEE VASQUEZ

When was your home built?

VF: The building dates back to the seventeenth century.

What is its history?

VF: The building is located in the first arrondissement, between the Palais-Royal and the Opéra. Jacques-Bénigne Bossuet, the court preacher to Louis XIV, spent the last years of his life in this building. Now the area is known as the Petit Tokyo of Paris because of the large Japanese community. At night, people flock to our neighborhood for the Japanese restaurants and cool bars.

When did it become yours?

VF: We decided to transform the space into a home in 2010. By that time, it had been one hundred years since the space had been used as a residence. My grandfather Pierre Frey had originally purchased the space to use as a fabric workshop, and later it served as an internal Pierre Frey museum, where we stored more than ten thousand historical fabrics and carpet samples.

What drew you to your home? What do you love most about it?

VF: I recall visiting the workshop as a child. I was always remember being intrigued by it and hoped to one day turn it into my own home. My grandfather would always tell me stories about the building and how it was so rich in French history, being built in the seventeenth century, one of the first buildings in the area. So when I returned to Paris, after living in Hong Kong for some time, I took on the renovations.

How have you put your mark on it?

VF: This is our first apartment together so it was very difficult for us to find a happy medium between our opposing styles. Luckily, we did have one thing in common! We are both eco-conscious and appreciate sustainable design. We also wanted a lot of color and only natural fibers, especially linen, organic cotton, and bamboo.

There are no true references when coming up with the interior design; our aesthetic is simply a mix of our diverse backgrounds. My French background created a liking for classic French paintings, design furniture, and toile de Jouy fabrics. With her Cuban-Ecuadorian origins, Bianca tends to be attracted to bold colors, streamlined architecture, and the 1930s Miami art deco scene. The apartment is a fusion of these two contrasting backgrounds, thus creating a retro-modern home with light touches of French classicism.

Where do you look for decor inspiration?

VF: We find inspiration at design fairs, during our travels, at my grandmother's house. We got the idea to make our coffee table after seeing a similar version at the Martin Margiela pop-up store in Milan. But often the greatest inspiration comes from the images you have in your head of how you remember home.

What are your favorite shops or sources for furnishings?

VF: The RA Antwerp boutique, Decades in North Miami Beach, and the online marketplace Deconet.com.

For decorative objects?

VF: Puces de Saint-Ouen [Porte de Cligancourt], Paris.

For art?

VF: School Gallery, Paris.

Do you have any favorites amongst the Pierre Frey textile Collection?

VF: The toile de Jouy Oberkampf in the dining room—I am French, so of course I have a toile de Jouy in my home! It was the first fabric we chose for the apartment.

How would you describe the use of color in your home?

VF: I enjoy color. It evokes emotions, so we use a lot of it at home.

What is your favorite place to spend time in your home, and what do you do there?

VF: We both agree that the kitchen is our favorite room. It really is the center of the apartment, open to all rooms, and where we always end up staying when we entertain friends at home. We spend most of our time there.

How would you describe the French approach to the details of a home?

VF: This is difficult to answer since everyone is different. If I were to choose one commonality, it would be that the French are known to be comfortable and confident with their style, and that shows in our interiors. We also have a long history of design, so even a modern decor will often have an element of classic design, most notably from the architecture.

Cool blue and white hues give this bedroom a nearly monochromatic look. The modern dot pattern in the "Circus" fabric by Jim Thompson used for the drapes perfectly complements the clean lines of the Saarinen Tulip chair, the cushion of which is covered in another dot pattern, "Dora," by Pierre Frey. The Joakim Eneroth photo on the wall unites the color scheme. There are literally countless shades of white interior paint available. Choosing the right one may be difficult, but pairing white with various tones of that color can transform it from clinical to comforting.

PRECEDING SPREAD This home's towering dining room offers views into other rooms on both the first and second floors. From the black-and-white space, the bright pastel blue chairs and red sofa in the living room are visible. Above, the parted draperies reveal the master bedroom. The openings add to the flow of the home's open plan.

ABOVE A vintage lamp by Raak peeks down from an upper level to illuminate the tempered-glass kitchen by Valcucine, with its rough hardwood floor. Steel barstools tuck in beneath the pale wooden countertop, facing the inky black script detail on the island. A vase full of wheat and Pierre Frey teacup trays give a subtle nod to the room's function.

BELOW At first glance, the sitting room appears to excel in simplicity, but the details of the room are quite complex. Various iterations of black and white frame the room, including the Braquenié rug; drapes in a vertical stripe, which elongate the room; and a ceiling with a grid of white beams. Still, the sofa, covered in vibrant red Pierre Frey fabric, and the Jacques Charpentier chairs in pale-blue wool Pierre Frey fabric take center stage. The clear acrylic of the chairs is echoed in an improvised coffee table, assembled from a glass tabletop placed on stacks of magazines.

Let your library spill out of the shelves. Embrace piles of books on the floor, under a table, anywhere they look good to you.

This all-white bathroom includes a freestanding tub, as well as a modern shower behind a glass wall, a collection of the homeowner's own prints and photos in white frames, and a Saarinen chair that boasts a shock of color, thanks to lipstick-red dotted "Dora" fabric by Pierre Frey on the cushion.

OPPOSITE A small corner is a showcase for bold, botanical green-and-white wallpaper and an Angle chair by Julian Mayor. White roman shades with bright-yellow trim filter the light. Piles of colorful books give the small but airy library a sense of life.

ART AND FURNISHINGS
L'ART ET L'AMEUBLEMENT

The frequency with which art and antique furnishings appear in the French home might be attributable to France's long history. People who are part of an old culture may have a more natural appreciation for the past and a keen awareness of the future and the way things evolve over time. Among the French, it's a sensibility that's shared across all ages and walks of life. Antiques aren't just for amateur historians, and art isn't just for collectors. Thanks in part to France's famous flea markets, anyone can access special and rare items, so these pieces turn up in all sorts of residences.

Homeowners exercise the freedom to use their beautiful finds however they please. Antiques aren't relegated to the living room alone; an antique bookcase placed in the master bathroom offers a surface for stacking towels, and in the kitchen, an apothecary-style table becomes undercounter storage. Fine art mingles with sketches, handwritten notes, and other framed ephemera, and all are displayed in an approachable, unmeticulous way. Hung on a wall, or leaning just so against one, artwork is equally easy to admire.

ABOVE With its fluid lines, Louise Bourgeois's *Eye to Eye* sculpture echoes the shape of the lamp made from a Sèvres porcelain vase, and contrasts with the geometric paneling on the wall and the sharp corners of the custom parchment-and-bronze side table.

BELOW A carved-wood chair and an oil painting make a tiny nook under the back stairwell of this home a focal point.

OPPOSITE Light and dark, smooth and coarse textures make each piece look more intriguing. The sophistication of a Jean-Michel Frank chair emphasizes the roughness of Christo's *Nine Packed Bottles* atop a white pedestal. The light colors of the chair and rug make the Mark Rothko *Two Greens with Red Stripe* hung on the wall look even deeper.

PRECEDING SPREAD A French 1940s rosewood game table, with a pair of Emilio Terry chairs covered in Georges Le Manach silk velvet, is the perfect setting for a little friendly competition. The lamp was made from a Louis XVI–period gilded-wood candlestick with a custom-made lamp shade by Anne Sokolsky. An eighteenth-century print of *La balançoire*, by Fragonard, rests on the windowsill.

Wall art can take many forms. Consider hanging everyday objects with graphic appeal; vintage board games can add color and a playful look to any room.

ABOVE A nineteenth-century home's original pocket doors feature both carved-wood moldings and frosted-glass panes. On the other side of the doors, a cowhide rug tops the hardwood floors; a crystal chandelier with silk lamp shades hangs above. In the foreground, a vintage chair shows its age but, thanks to its fine craftsmanship, still looks glamorous.

PRECEDING SPREAD, LEFT In this living room, the furnishings offer both high design and plush comfort. A Castiglione lamp hangs over the French metal coffee table from Stéphane Olivier. Danish chairs from the 1960s, made of metal, wood, and leather, boast impressive structural details, while the sofa invites relaxation. Piles and shelves of books, a Christian Liaigre side table, and a backgammon board mounted on the wall complete the room.

PRECEDING SPREAD, RIGHT A light fixture made from the whisk attachment from a commercial mixer looks like a piece of art and receives pride of place in a stairwell.

OPPOSITE Custom-made barrel shades by Maxalto suspended above a Christian Liaigre dining table and nineteenth-century chairs offer drama in this eat-in kitchen.

COLLECTING À LA FRANÇAISE

THE FRENCH have a way of collecting and displaying their art and antiques that suggests effortlessness. It seems as if each incredible item in their homes has been in the family for years, and on a whim they placed it against that wall, or by that window, with an intimidating mixture of stylish imprecision and familiarity with very fine things. The French are simply comfortable with collecting and with perusing their famous flea markets and antiques shops. In fact, anyone with an interest in vintage, estate, or antique things can have success in shopping the secondary market by discerning between simple and complex purchases:

SIMPLE PURCHASES If an item catches your eye while you're shopping, traveling, or even browsing the Internet, ask yourself two questions: "Do I love it?" and "Can I afford it?" If you answer yes to both questions, it is a purchase you will not regret.

COMPLEX PURCHASES If you're evaluating an investment piece, or you're after an authentic item from a certain period, do as much research as you can. Investigate the quality of the item, relative to others like it, and determine whether the price the vendor is asking seems low, high, or about right. If your research reveals that the piece is of good quality at an appropriate price, bring it home.

A Napoléon III cabinet painted black and flanked by a pair of nineteenth-century Scottish chairs is an imposing presence; the surrounding curiosities—gazelle horns and framed scarabs—add intrigue. This chest was retrofitted to accommodate a modern media center; the doors keep all the blinking lights and power cords elegantly concealed.

OPPOSITE A cluster of black, white, and grey framed items show that wall art need not be fine art. The warm colors of a walnut Swedish-modern chest of drawers from the 1950s contrast with the cool tones above, as well as with the industrial-looking chrome Buquet lamp.

Bring the outdoors in. Use great-looking garden furniture in a formal setting to complement even the most intricate antique.

OPPOSITE A custom Balinese carved-wood door is visible beyond the rustic kitchen door; the placement and uniqueness of the door make it a decorative object in its own right.

PRECEDING SPREAD, LEFT Periods intermingle to create an original interior: art nouveau–inspired wrought-iron chairs, a buffet with a Directoire look, and an antique center-pedestal table. Crystal candlesticks litter the mantel.

ABOVE An American farmhouse table and chairs are topped by a Czech art-glass light fixture, an exquisite conversation piece for any dinner party. Along the wall, a French industrial piece acts as a buffet; the 1970s French lamp texture and style provides a contrast. An Indian painting between the room's windows pulls together the colors in the room.

PRECEDING SPREAD, RIGHT This kitchen's French-country armoire and copper cookware, found at a flea market, are enlivened a bit by the addition of a crane from legendary taxidermy shop Deyrolle and lime-green paint on the walls and doors.

A SHOPPER'S HISTORY OF FRENCH INTERIOR DESIGN

If you take an interest in a specific period, there are innumerable references available that will allow you to immerse yourself in that era's styles. If, instead, you're only interested in learning enough to speak the language of the antiques shops and flea markets, here is the simplest possible history of French interior design:

DATES/PERIOD	HIGHLIGHTS
A.D. 1150–1550 MIDDLE AGES, GOTHIC, MEDIEVAL	Materials used were wood, ceramics, stone, and plaster. Furniture included heavy, simple wooden stools, benches, trestle tables, and chests. Windows were small for increased security and because glass was unavailable or rare. Doors were made from vertical boards secured with horizontal battens and metal straps. Lancet arches were common in doors and windows. Where wooden floors existed, they were of the wide-plank variety.
1450–1600 RENAISSANCE	Italian artists were hired by the king, bringing the Renaissance to France. Architecture and design reflected both Gothic design and the influence of classical antiquity. Frescoes and carved and inlaid panels were introduced. Herringbone floors appeared.
1600–1715 BAROQUE, LOUIS XIII, LOUIS XIV	Stucco, gilding, and painting were prominently used in decor, as seen at Versailles. Technical advances made mirrors more common. "French windows" appeared. Veneered wood, brass, pewter, and horn were used in furniture. Chairs were increasingly upholstered. Beds were draped with fabric. The commode, or chest of drawers, was introduced in the Louis XIV period. An Asian influence emerged, marking the beginning of chinoiserie.
1700–1760 ROCOCO, RÉGENCE, LOUIS XV	Carved, paneled walls and classical designs carried over from the baroque period. Wood furniture was carved, lacquered, veneered, or embellished with marquetry. Bronze was frequently used. Chairs had curved lines, different from the square lines of the Louis XVI period. Eastern influences continued.

DATES/PERIOD	HIGHLIGHTS
1760–1789 EARLY NEOCLASSIC, LOUIS XVI	Mahogany and other exotic woods, as well as a variety of metals, gained in popularity. Louis XVI chair backs did not attach to seats; joints were well defined. The *secrétaire*, or drop-front desk, became popular.
1789–1820 LATE NEOCLASSIC, DIRECTOIRE, EMPIRE	Furniture relied on more-strict interpretations of classical design. Moldings were rarely used; walls were flat. Chair crests rolled back in an S-shape. Console tables and center tables were common.
1815–1870 REVIVAL, RESTORATION, SECOND EMPIRE	The Industrial Revolution's machine production began to replace craftsmen. Designs were inspired by those of the previous centuries, as far back as the Middle Ages. In homes, designs of different periods began to be mixed together. Tufted upholstery was popular due to the emphasis on comfort.
1890–1920 ART NOUVEAU	Plant forms and curved lines defined this time. Highly decorative ironwork was popular. Gothic, Japanese, and German styles became influential.
1920–1940 ART DECO	Styles reflected simplified art nouveau designs and the increasingly industrialized world. Sharp angles and bold geometric designs characterized this period. Rich and exotic materials were important.
1945–1970 INTERNATIONAL MODERN	Simplicity, function, and utility were emphasized over ornament. Steel, chrome, leather, plywood, and plastic were used in a wide variety of styles.

ABOVE A watercolor print by Mark Rothko hangs in a white stairwell to be viewed in ascent and descent. The angular frame highlights the curvilinear stairwell.

BELOW A crystal chandelier hangs from a trompe l'oeil ceiling at the center of a highly adorned room; a Directoire-period desk topped with mirrored obelisks and an antique vase, with an eighteenth-century watercolor of a French Revolutionary soldier hung above, sits beside the fireplace.

Place beauty anywhere. Art may get even more attention if it's in an unexpected spot. In a stairwell, the lack of distractions makes the work even more impressive.

Create an organic and
appealing flow of artwork
with a collection of
framed ephemera, such
as photos, sketches, and
handwritten notes.

elegate your
es to the living
nly. They'll be
ore striking
nventional
s such as the
om, dressing
closet, or
.

Flood a table with candles—pillars, tapers, and votives—to create an unpredictable centerpiece. As they burn, the melting wax renders an evolving sculpture.

ABOVE A Louis XV chair sits beneath an appealingly askew sconce. The chair's new upholstery and nail-head detailing update the classic look. (In the evening, the sconce glows with light from its wax candles.)

BELOW An oversized wooden bathtub is reminiscent of the medieval period. Gauzy curtains soften the look.

OPPOSITE The lacquered top of the extremely rare 1940s Maison Jansen Louis XV–style dining table reflects the candlelight, setting the room aglow. The chairs are also designed in the Louis XV style and are covered in a grey cotton by Pierre Frey.

PRECEDING SPREAD, LEFT This foyer, with its panoramic "L'Hindustan" wallpaper by Zuber and a kilim rug, proves that art can take many forms within a home. The exotic and impressive wallpaper and rug have contrasting patterns, but the vivid colors immediately captivate all who enter.

PRECEDING SPREAD, RIGHT The master bathroom is an unexpected but lovely home for antiques. A Napoléon III bibliothèque from 1860 is reincarnated as a linen closet to house crisp all-white towels and sheets. An occasional chair of the same period, a piece typically used now and then in a living room or sitting room, is cleverly relocated to the bath. An exhaust fan can prevent moisture from damanaging sensitive items.

In a space with many entrances and exits, cover a doorway with artwork to make the room feel more intimate and self-contained.

TO HANG OR TO LEAN

FRAMED ARTWORKS are intended to be displayed against a wall, but their arrangement is up to you. If you prefer to hang your art, a piece can stand alone or with other items. The appeal of positioning a single frame on the wall is that it becomes a focal point. A cluster looks more abundant. Done right, a grouping of wall art will balance consistency and diversity: one element should be constant throughout all of the pieces, whether it's a color in the art or the frames, or the material or texture of the frames; this allows you to create an eclectic suite that still seems pulled together.

For a looser, stylishly irreverent look, consider simply leaning your art against the wall on a mantel, a table, or even the floor. While a large-scale work may lean on its own, clustering is more important with smaller items to keep them looking clever and intentional as opposed to inadvertent.

If you choose to lean your artworks, make sure to secure them to the floor or wall with museum wax, double-sided tape, or hook and nail to protect them from accidental damage.

OPPOSITE A rarely used doorway doubles as wall space for a painting from the eighteenth century.

A black-and-gilt Napoléon III chair covered in Pierre Frey taffeta is striking against the black-stained floor and beside eighteenth-century prints in black frames, perched against the wall.

FRENCH FRAME OF MIND

One of the most inspiring things about French decorating is the way in which homeowners display any item they find interesting or attractive as if it were art, hanging or leaning it just so against a wall as if it were a masterpiece. In addition to the rule-bending confidence inherent in these wall displays, their success is attributable to the frames around the art and the ephemera. Framing is a nuanced skill that can be as artful as the paintings, photos, or prints that are its raison d'être. It serves many purposes: first and foremost to display cherished images, but also to enhance their appearance and to shelter them from atmospheric conditions that can cause degradation over time. A professional framer has the discerning eye and experience that allows him to compose a custom frame from a few simple elements in order to make the work shine, to draw out its subtly appealing details, and to complement your decor. These days, there are also many websites that allow shoppers to create their own frames à la carte. Here's a bit of information to help you make an educated purchase, whether your frame will be professionally made or DIY:

CHOOSE YOUR FRAME The first decision regards wood versus metal. Wood is conventionally thought best for a traditional piece, while metal has been recommended for contemporary works. However, there are now so many different looks and finishes in both wood and metal that it's no longer appropriate to label one classic and the other current, and the choice really boils down to personal taste.

CONSIDER MATTING Thought of as optional, and traditionally omitted with paintings on canvas, matting is used to separate the framed item from the glazing (glass) to prevent the two from adhering to each other due to moisture and tem-

perature fluctuations. There's a decorative purpose to matting, too, in that mats create a border between the image and the frame. Though mats are available in all the colors of the rainbow, mats are most often selected in shades of off-white, cream, and beige because those tones are flattering to most images.

MULL THE MAT'S WIDTH Professional framers determine the width of the matting based on the size of the image and that of its focal point. They may even customize the mat to be wider at the bottom than it is at the top—an effect referred to as weighting—to bring the focal point nearer the center of the frame. If you are creating your own frame, consider a mat that is double the width of the frame for an appealing look that suits most images.

ADD A LAYER Mats can be layered to create an additional, thinner border between the outer mat and the image. The inner mat may be the same color as the outer one, adding depth to the composite of the frame. Alternatively, you may choose an inner mat in a color that appears in the image in order to enhance its appearance.

OPT FOR QUALITY MATS Whatever color, number, or width of mats you choose, be sure to select an acid-free variety. Untreated wood-pulp mats have naturally occurring acidity that will cause mats and art to discolor and deteriorate. Instead, seek out either 100 percent cotton ragmat, or more-affordable acid-free wood-pulp matting for your frame.

LOOK INTO A LINER If you are framing stretched canvas, you may want to add a linen liner, which is a narrow wooden frame wrapped in fabric. Similar in function to matting, linen liners create a border between the canvas and the frame, adding visual interest and, thanks to the weave of the linen, additional texture to the frame.

DEBATE GLAZING Intended to preserve the integrity of an image, *glazing* refers to the pane of glass used in a frame; most often, it is omitted for framed canvases, unless the work is extremely vulnerable to atmospheric changes. There are several types of glazing, some of which offer reduced or zero reflectiveness, or protection from the sun's damaging ultraviolet rays. Some framers offer acrylic glazing, which is less fragile than glass but can create static electricity, which is not recommended for delicate pieces, such as charcoal drawings. Generally, cost increases as do protective features, and some of the treated-glass varieties may have slight differences in clarity or color, all of which will guide your choice of glass to top off your frame.

1. CLASSIC

2. MODERN 3. MODERN

4. CLASSIC 5. CLASSIC

6. CLASSIC

7. CLASSIC 8. CLASSIC

9. ORNATE

10. CLASSIC 11. CLASSIC

REFRESHING AND REHABBING

YOU'VE FOUND a piece you love on the secondary or resale market, whether at an antiques store, a flea market, or a consignment shop. Now you can start to think about whether it needs work. Before you make an additional investment of time or money, consider both the aesthetics of the item and how you will use it in your home:

- If it will function as decor only, you may choose to leave the item as you found it, imperfections and all. This might apply to an antique chair that's a little wobbly or has worn wood, leather, or upholstery. Display it like a piece of art in your home; a little wear and tear can make it more interesting.

- If it will be lightly used, consider easy updates, such as new hardware or a fresh coat of paint. For example, if you find a beautiful secondhand bedside table, you may rest books, a lamp, and other objects on top of it, but if you won't necessarily need to get in and out of its drawers frequently, simply freshening the exterior of the piece will be more than sufficient.

- If it's an item that will be used daily or is weight bearing, such as seat furniture, a dining table, or a chest of drawers, more thorough rehabilitation may be required to make it safe and durable. Examine the structure of the piece to see what kind of repairs might be in order: Check the legs, stretchers, seat, and armrests of chairs; the pedestal, legs, or trestle of a table; or the drawer runners of a dresser to ensure easy opening and closing. Give sofas and chairs new life by restuffing their cushions and re-covering them with new upholstery. The more intensive the work is, the higher cumulative price tag the piece will carry, but if you really want to live with your antique or vintage furniture, it's money well spent.

OPPOSITE Pleasant tension arises between rustic antler lamps and a sartorial collection of the homeowner's custom-made shirt collars atop an antique worktable of mysterious, unknown origins. A seventeenth-century Korean vase filled with flowers adds a sensual note.

Beside a Belgian iron urn, a Napoléon III *chaise de bal* is adorned with original silk fabric.

Think creatively about wall space. In a room with unconventional dimensions, even a pitched ceiling can be a vehicle to display art.

BELOW Jasper Johns's *Map* above the custom-designed banquette sofa by Kristen McGinnis gives this room a serene look. The Jean-Charles Moreaux coffee table is topped with a Chinese bronze piece from the Shang Dynasty and Franz West's *Paßstück*.

OPPOSITE The rounded lines of the Le Corbusier chaise contrast nicely with the right angles of the paneled French doors and intricate classical moldings and trim.

PRECEDING SPREAD, LEFT A French chair from the late nineteenth century creates a dramatic, eclectic arrangement with a Chinese lacquer screen from earlier in that century.

PRECEDING SPREAD, RIGHT A nineteenth-century English chest of drawers surrounded by an Italian gilt mirror from the same era, rosewood-and-tarnished gold Maison Jansen chairs re-covered in Brunschwig & Fils velvet, and a set of neoclassical accessories from Marc Philippe, Paris, illustrate how elegantly European and Asian designs complement one another.

BRIGITTE LANGEVIN AND MARC HISPARD

When was your home built?

MH: Our flat is in a house that was built at the beginning of the twentieth century.

When did it become yours?

MH: We have lived here for five years.

What drew you to your home? What do you love most about it?

MH: I saw an advertisement in the newspaper, and I went to look at it. It was in a perfect spot for us to live. When I saw the apartment, it was empty, with full white walls, and that was it. I liked the idea of how one room flows into the next—we can enjoy the look from every room to the next—and the height of the ceiling (almost fourteen feet).

BL: I love the design of the rooms, and that the library is round. It's in the best area of Paris, in Saint-Germain-des-Prés.

How have you put your mark on it?

MH: We decided to leave the apartment white, and with the furniture we put in, the white walls were okay for us.

What are your favorite shops?

BL: In Paris, I love the antiques shop Alexandre Biaggi in the Rue de Seine—they have the most beautiful antiques. Patrick Fourtin is another favorite antiques dealer. Olivier Watelet is an excellent source for furnishings and accents.

Do you have any favorite pieces of artwork?

BL: I like all of what we have. For one, the black-and-white African mask by the window—I love

this one. The Philippe Pasqua in the salon is another favorite of mine. We've had it for two years. We found it at an exhibition. We like to go to the galleries and meet people, and when we see something we like, we buy it. We don't buy things so expensive, but they often have more value later.

How have you acquired the pieces in your collection?

MH: We bought the paintings, furniture, art, and objects all over the years. It's eclectic; we like art in many forms, and we did buy all over the world. We travel a lot, and sometimes we find things for our home as we travel. To be a fashion photographer, you always have your eye looking at something, searching for something.

Do you have a favorite period in interior design?

BL: I like the forties, fifties, sixties. I like the classic things, like from Knoll—Saarinen tables and chairs. I am not so particular, though. It's mixed.

Do any of your furnishings stand out as favorites?

BL: The Le Corbusier is a very, very special old chair. We have had it for twenty years. It's classic, like the Pipistrello lamp. It can last for years and years, and in twenty years it will still be good.

What is your favorite place to spend time in your home, and what do you do there?

MH: My favorite place is my office, from where I can look to the living room and the library. My wife's favorite is everywhere, in particular the kitchen—she is a very good cook.

BL: The library. I don't like the idea of a dining room. I like dinner in the library. We take all the books off the table and we have dinner there with friends. If we are six or four, we have dinner on this table. If we have more, we have a round piece of wood we put on top of the table. I keep it under the bed and take it out when we need it. We always use the fireplace in the library, and we light the candles on the chandelier. In France, you cook much more than in New York. Here, you cook very often. I do one or two dinners a week with friends. I don't like to have too many people. That way you can talk.

How would you describe the French approach to the details of a home?

BL: I think it's mixed, elegant. You can have something old with something very modern. It's something Parisian. It's something evident, elegant, eclectic. Modern and ancient. You don't buy something because it will be nice with other things. You buy it because you like it, and it's something special. You buy what you like, and everything goes very well and fits together. Voilà.

Arrange your book collection by hue. Remove the book jackets if you want solid colors; keep the jackets on if you like a more graphic or patterned effect.

PRECEDING SPREAD A cluster of fine objects turns an easily overlooked space between two stunning windows into something noteworthy. The table is a creation of Maxine Old, a French decorator popular in the 1940s; it is topped by a model of the atelier of Francis Bacon by Charles Matton, an African mask, animal horns, and a 1940s lamp, all crowned by a Philippe Pasqua work hanging on the wall.

This room lives a double life: it's a library by day and a place to enjoy home-cooked French meals with friends in the evening. The space is glamorous in a pleasantly haphazard way. A crystal chandelier hangs low over the green marble-topped table, set with two chrome-and-moleskin chairs from the 1940s, where the homeowners share meals when dining in. Even with the unexpected combination of white walls and white draperies, the room has a rich look, thanks to the profusion of objects on every surface. The sharp angles of the bookcase emphasize the uniqueness of the oval room.

OBJECTS AND ACCENTS

LES OBJETS ET LES ORNEMENTS

Decorative accents are a critical layer in French homes. Accents are syn-onymous with a French term, *objets d'art,* referring to anything with aesthetic value that doesn't quite fall under the heading of "art." They fill in the gaps in decor and make a house look finished and feel lived in. More is more, so long as they are displayed with a curatorial eye that keeps them from tripping over the line into clutter. Perhaps most important, accents make each home unique because, individually and together, they keenly reflect the personality of its owners. In French homes, accents are displayed in a thoughtful yet haphazard way. Animal figurines act as doorstops; Hermès boxes are arranged into an orange obelisk; books are sometimes piled neatly, sometimes askew; and taxidermied animals infuse a natural element. The combinations are as remarkable as the homes themselves.

For an interesting wall collection, hang clocks in a group. They can be set to the time zones of your favorite places, or not tell time at all.

BELOW A nineteenth-century French mahogany bookcase is a perfect display for the homeowner's Venetian-glass bottles from the same era, a neo-Greek terra-cotta urn, and a pair of Dutch lamps, with an antique French Empire mirror hanging above.

OPPOSITE This vintage brass bar cart is stocked with a mixed collection of Saint-Louis crystal, including both the Amadeus and Tommy patterns; the juxtaposition of the two patterns makes each more striking. The reflections on the glass add luster to any room.

PRECEDING SPREAD An easily forgotten corner becomes a focal point thanks to a collection of futurist and cubist works by Kazimir Malevich, Albert Gleizes, and artists from the school of Fernand Léger. A wrought-iron stool holds art tomes and an urn dating back to Ancient Greece. Animal figurines from homeowner and decorator Brigitte Langevin's collection act as clever doorstops, drawing the eye from high to low.

Take your beautiful china, crystal,
and serving pieces out of the cabinets
and let them adorn your home.

BOOKS OF WONDER

FRENCH DECORATING emphasizes uniqueness, and yet there are certain constants; books are among the most apparent. Books serve many purposes. In reading them, we may be inspired, transported, entertained, educated, provoked, called to action, calmed, soothed, or made thoughtful. Books aid us in work, and please us in leisure. In this increasingly digital age, the physical form of books is evolving, but especially in French decorating, a love of the printed and bound volume remains.

In French homes, books are used as decor. They are piled on a side table or just so beside a chair or a bed. They are used to support a tabletop for a one-of-a-kind coffee table. They are set out in such a way that the hues of the books' jackets have a major impact on the color scheme of the room. Much-loved novels mix with glossy art and fashion tomes as well as vintage books purchased chiefly for the look of their leather bindings. Bookshelves become major statements, but even within them, the books are arranged in an unexpected way. Let these homes inspire you to keep growing your book collection, and consider some creative ways to make books a compelling aspect of your decor:

PLAY WITH PLACEMENT Experiment with the way the books are oriented within the shelves; line them up vertically, or stack them in horizontal piles. Position some books with their spines out, and others with their spines in.

LET THEIR INNER BEAUTY SHOW To add texture to your shelves, remove the dust jackets to display your books' cloth or paper covers.

COLOR-CODE THEM Arrange the books by the dominant color, either with the jackets off or with them on.

CREATE YOUR OWN JACKETS Fashion your own book jackets out of white or brown kraft paper, wallpaper, or any type of decorative sheets.

With books facing in and out, white and ivory pages contrast nicely with colorful bindings and covers for a dynamic look.

A horizontal "stack" of objects creates a multilayered image, with an industrial-style table lamp and a vintage vase of flowers in the foreground, an American folk art horse, an empty frame, and, on top, a mother-of-pearl sconce.

OPPOSITE Art and fashion books and magazines act as decor stacked on a plywood-and-antique column console. The frenzy of books is very appealing; the ones lining the exposed brick wall give the visual effect of wallpaper.

If you feel bold and have a giant collection of books, pile them, cluster them, let it be natural. Use books as objects to make your home feel lived in.

FLOWERS AND FOLIAGE

FRESH FLOWERS and houseplants are a lush finishing touch for any room. They offer excellent opportunities to showcase a special vase, pot, or urn, and whether they last a week or many years, they are evolving accessories, subtly changing over time. In addition to their aesthetic value, flowers and plants have been shown to improve mood and productivity as well as air quality. Choosing cut flowers to enhance your home is easy, since you have to live with your decision for only a matter of days, but selecting the right houseplant requires more thought. Here are a few things to consider if you'd like to add indoor plants to your interiors:

LIGHT Try to gauge the amount of sunlight a plant would receive in each place you'd like to put one. You can find a beautiful variety to suit low- or high-light areas, and plenty that will thrive between the two extremes.

MAINTENANCE Are you likely to meticulously care for your plant, or are you more likely to occasionally forget to water it? Be honest about your interest and ability to maintain your plant, and let that help guide your decision, too.

GROWTH Finally, consider whether you would like a slow-growing plant that can stay in the same location and container for years, or if you are game for repotting it and changing its location as it expands.

OPPOSITE A 1930s mirrored side table sits beside the upholstered bed. Orange Hermès gift boxes stacked on the floor look like a sculpture. The red parrot tulips on the bedside table look as if painted in oils.

Bicycles tucked beneath a canopy of ivy and terra-cotta-potted plants help decorate the exterior of a Parisian home. Vintage bicycles make for beautiful decorative objects inside or out; find them at antiques shops or flea markets.

If you love a chandelier that is not a functional light fixture, hang it beside recessed lighting, so that you can take advantage of the beauty of the piece and still get the lighting you need.

ABOVE One of a pair of sconces with beaded shades looks brilliant against a blue wall. The slightly off-kilter quality makes it even more appealing.

BELOW Taxidermy is wired and then electrified to create lamps and then mixed in with a cluster of silver serving pieces; the faint shine of the animal horns echoes the reflection on the silver.

OPPOSITE A suite of pieces creates a dramatic entryway from a small section of wall space. An English settee is covered in vintage leopard fabric; an African tribal stool sits beside it, piled high with books.

PRECEDING SPREAD, LEFT Above this kitchen sink, an antique Asian urn is displayed on an 1880s plaster wall bracket recovered from a church; the large, dark urn looks especially dramatic sitting high above the white-and-soft-blue cabinetry and neutral-hued stone counters and backsplash.

PRECEDING SPREAD, RIGHT This dining room has a stylish farmhouse motif, thanks to the wrought-iron chairs, antique chest, and chandelier. Botanical prints hang on the wall above a table topped with a champagne cooler repurposed as a planter.

WILDLIFE ART

TAXIDERMY GREW out of the prehistoric practice of treating animal hides to be used for clothing and shelter. Crude stuffed animal forms eventually evolved into highly sophisticated mounts, on which each element of an animal's physiology is correctly displayed in an attractive posture. Whereas in the United States, taxidermy evokes images of rustic hunting lodges, in France it has a more glamorous image, associated with everything from exotic birds and butterflies to giraffes and tigers, and is appreciated as an art form. Deyrolle, a famous taxidermy shop in Paris, has been selling the mounts that appear in many of the finest homes in France since 1831. It is frequented by both locals and visitors for its museum-quality and exotic wares. The shop itself may be partially responsible for the endearment of taxidermy in France.

In the French home, taxidermy blends nature and art, creating wildly glamorous artifacts. Here in the United States, there are many laws governing taxidermy, and they vary from state to state, making animal mounts very hard to come by in some places. If you love the look and can't acquire a collection of preserved animals, consider the wide variety of replicas available in plaster, stone, metal, or even plastic. They will help you capture the chic style so common in French interiors.

Japanese metal cranes from the nineteenth century pose beside a nineteenth-century French chair of painted wood, covered in velvet. The fine lines of the crane sculptures highlight the carved-wood bones of the chair.

OPPOSITE At the bedside is a console table topped with a vintage lamp found at a Paris flea market, a mounted bird, and a Burmese temple box. Above, a charcoal drawing by Yvan Guillaume picks up on their jet-black finishes.

A crystal chandelier and millinery accessories give this master bedroom a romantic mood. Whitewashed armoires line the back wall; lamps behind the bed take the form of busts of Madame Bovary, whimsically topped with hats for lamp shades. Hatboxes and hat stands add to the look. Built-in shelving flanking the armoires hidden by white curtains hung from wrought-iron rails provides the perfect storage for shoes.

PRECEDING SPREAD, LEFT In the corner of this living room, items collected at various places and times are delightfully displayed. A large metal gate is made over as a mirror with an antique chandelier mounted on it. At the foot of the mirror are candlesticks and framed art, which leans against a white wrought-iron rail and a bronze-and-blue mosaic tile wall.

PRECEDING SPREAD, RIGHT A marble-and-plaster console of the homeowner's own design provides a staging area for French art deco glass lamps, Jeremy Kost's photo *It's Always Darkest Before Dawn* (leaning), a plaster bust wearing a necklace, a vintage ceramic vase, and other curios. An abstract print by John Carter is surrounded by a crucifix, a metal *milagro* (or spiritual charm), and a hand-shaped hook holding a collection of jewelry. The different sizes, materials, and unconventional placement offer plenty of entertainment for the eye.

MINIATURE MONUMENTS

NOW POPULAR as decorative accents in French homes, obelisks were invented by the ancient Egyptians as massive, sacred objects that towered above ceremonial sites and temples. The four-sided tapered pillars topped with pyramid-shaped points are believed to have been designed to resemble a ray of sunlight, and bore the names and images of the pharaohs who erected them, so that the obelisks in effect raised the pharaohs up to the heavens. Because of this symbolism and because obelisks were built at the height of the Egyptian civilization, the monuments came to represent power, glory, and imperialism, and so have been coveted and copied by other civilizations ever since.

So coveted were they that though twenty-one ancient Egyptian obelisks are still standing, only five remain in Egypt. One obelisk built by Ramses the Great during the thirteenth century BC is now located in Paris's Place de la Concorde, and is an iconic part of the city's skyline. New York City's Central Park boasts one of Tuthmosis III's obelisks (the other is in London), nicknamed Cleopatra's Needle, but perhaps the most famous obelisk-shaped structure in the United States is the nineteenth-century Washington Monument.

The appeal of small-scale obelisks in interior design certainly has something to do with their powerful connotations. In French homes, they may simply stand as a totem of the city of Paris, and though Freudian types may point to still other symbolism, it's probably true that for many designers and homeowners, the sharp angles and tapering height of obelisks simply add interesting dimensions to interiors. Traditionally rendered in marble or granite, obelisks are also made from such rare stones as quartz, rock crystal, and malachite. Contemporary reproductions made from mirrors, wood, porcelain, and even cement offer a range of styles and price points that make obelisks an appealing addition to any home.

A trio of a George III ostrich egg on a silver stand, an Italian-stone obelisk, and a china demitasse with saucer grace the white marble mantel; showcasing the cup and saucer out of the context of dining allows its fine details to shine.

Let your objects reflect your life, experiences, and personality. Collect items while traveling, whether to another city or another country; this will add character to your home.

ABOVE Shapes are juxtaposed for visual interest. The geometric grid in the Les Carrés carpet by Braquenié makes the helter-skelter split shelves by Peter Marigold look all the more artful. The spherical forms of the vintage lamps by Raak harmonize with the curves of the Marco Zanuso Lady chair, covered in a Pierre Frey fabric.

BELOW A Czech art-glass chandelier has a look that's part art deco, part medieval.

OPPOSITE A striking Arctic Pear chandelier from Ochre with a four-foot span hangs from this living room's pressed-metal ceiling, reflecting natural light during the day.

PRECEDING SPREAD The French doors lead from one beautiful room into the next. Beyond the Caravane sofa and through the doorway flanked by école de Fernand Léger drawings, an oversized African mask and low-hanging crystal chandelier from Jean-Paul Beaujard Paris invite a closer look at the dining room.

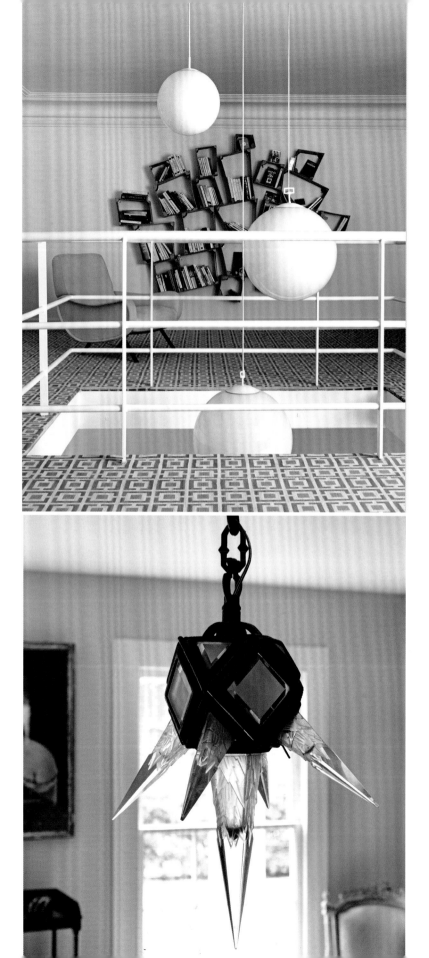

A DELICATE BALANCE

THE WAY the French use objects is certainly one of the most striking elements of their decor. Shapes, sizes, textures, and colors are mixed. Trying to pinpoint the way these interesting items are displayed is difficult—in some interiors, it's neat; in others, it's artistically haphazard. The quality that unites these arrangements and makes them so successful is balance.

Balance is related to symmetry, but it's not quite the same thing. To create an appealing cluster of objects, you need not create a mirror-image effect, but rather use items of similar visual weight or density to create an even look. A lamp might be opposite a bust, or a crystal obelisk might counterpoise a vase of flowers, and with that balance established, any number of curios may be scattered among them, creating an intriguingly appealing look.

Give your objects maximum impact by displaying them en masse. The pieces do not need to match exactly; for example, you can use old, new, plaster, or wood antlers together to create this look.

The malachite boxes, candlestick, egg, and tray share a bright-green hue, but each object draws uniqueness from its own pattern of deep-green veins. Displaying them together makes both their similarities and differences more apparent.

OPPOSITE Through the rustic board-and-batten door, the foyer is lined with vintage hunting trophies. On one side, 1950s lamps and an eighteenth-century marquetry ebony wood box adorn a nineteenth-century console table. Opposite is a wrought-iron bench covered with David Hicks fabric. The highly decorated walls emphasize the full height of the space.

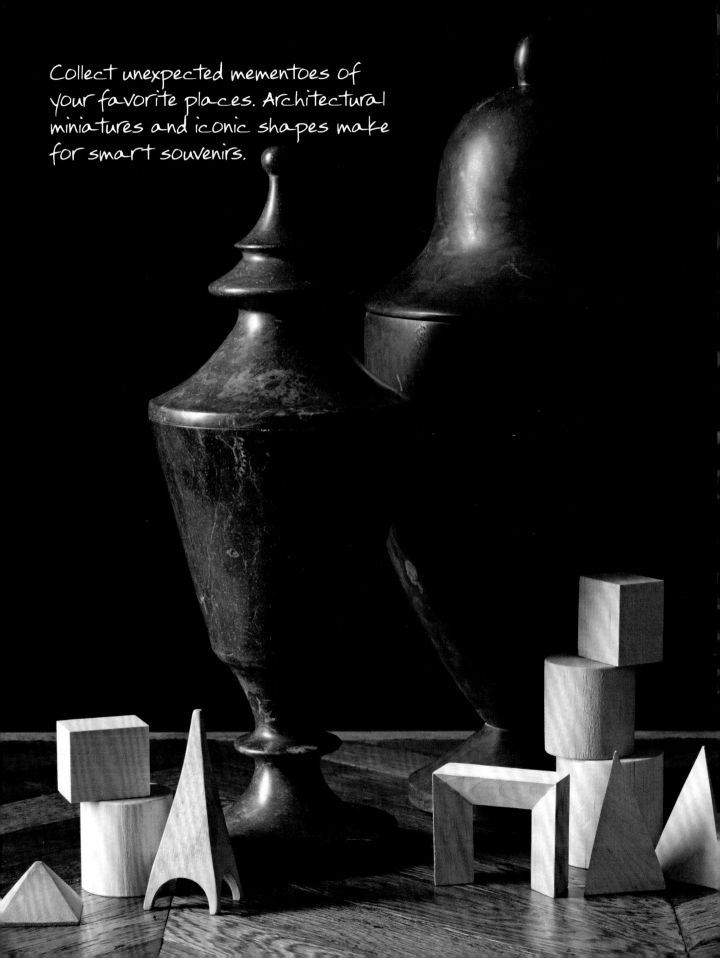

Collect unexpected mementoes of your favorite places. Architectural miniatures and iconic shapes make for smart souvenirs.

ABOVE Seen through a rectangular doorway with a transom above, the lancet window offers a glimpse of the home's architectural dynamism.

BELOW A spigot for a garden hose becomes a focal point with the addition of an embellished iron fountain.

OPPOSITE Flea-market finds, from a green glass bottle on the floor to vintage bowls and empty frames, create interest along a stone wall. A vintage olive jar fills a cutout in the wall above.

PRECEDING SPREAD, LEFT A rustic look emerges from a variety of antlers mounted on the wall. Anything clustered and contained within a frame often feels thoughtful and extremly artful. A trio of French side tables atop a bright-red Moroccan rug sit before an eighteenth-century Swedish daybed with a weathered finish.

PRECEDING SPREAD, RIGHT Black-marble urns by Oly have the city of Paris (rendered in wooden blocks) at their feet; the smooth surface and curved lines of the urns are striking beside the grain and sharp angles of the wooden pieces.

RECYCLED RICHES

THE MULTILAYERED STYLE of French interiors owes much to the country's famous flea markets. At the *brocantes*, furniture and art from all periods of design come back into circulation and are sold alongside recent creations, making the markets themselves a model for the eclecticism that defines French homes. Shoppers and collectors travel from all over the world to visit the Gallic markets, but there are excellent sources for antique, vintage, and estate pieces stateside as well. Here is a brief list of some of the best on both sides of the Atlantic:

Alameda Point Antiques and Collectibles Faire
WHERE: Alameda, California
WHEN: first Sunday of every month, 6 a.m. to 3 p.m.
KNOWN FOR: furniture, art, and decorative objects, all twenty years old or older

Brooklyn Flea
WHERE: Brooklyn, New York
WHEN: every weekend of the year, 10 a.m. to 3 p.m.
KNOWN FOR: antiques, vintage clothing and collectibles, local art and crafts, and food

Long Beach Outdoor Antique and Collectible Market
WHERE: Long Beach, California
WHEN: third Sunday of every month, 5:30 a.m. to 3 p.m.
KNOWN FOR: antiques and vintage collectibles

Marché aux Puces Saint-Ouen de Clignancourt
WHERE: 18th Arrondissement, Paris
WHEN: every Saturday to Monday, 9 a.m. to 6 p.m.
KNOWN FOR: reportedly the world's largest flea market, featuring items of every kind, from furniture to clothing to art; famous *marchés* within include Vernaison, Serpette, and Paul Bert

127 Corridor Sale
WHERE: U.S. Highway 127 between West Unity, Ohio, and Gadsden, Alabama
WHEN: first weekend in August; hours vary
KNOWN FOR: yard-sale items

Puces de Vanves
WHERE: 14th Arrondissement, Paris
WHEN: every Saturday and Sunday, 7 a.m. to 1 p.m.
KNOWN FOR: art, military items, vintage clothing, and decorative objects

Rose Bowl Flea Market
WHERE: Pasadena, California
WHEN: second Sunday of every month, 5 a.m. to 4:30 p.m.
KNOWN FOR: antiques, collectibles, furniture, clothing, and jewelry

Springfield Antique Show & Flea Market
WHERE: Springfield, Ohio
WHEN: various dates in January, March, April, May, July, August, September, October, and November
KNOWN FOR: antiques, collectibles, and bric-a-brac

Texas Antique Weekend
WHERE: several communities between Fayetteville and Carmine, Texas
WHEN: first weekend in April and first weekend in October; hours vary
KNOWN FOR: antiques, art, crafts, and collectibles

Treasure Mart
WHERE: Ann Arbor, Michigan
WHEN: Monday to Saturday, 9 a.m. to 3:30 p.m.
KNOWN FOR: antiques and collectibles sold on consignment

OPPOSITE Curios artfully clutter a nineteenth-century American side table; the strong vertical lines of the decorative pieces make the compact table a greater presence in the room.

Combine plants, such as potted herbs, with other objects to create a fresh, gardenlike feel among antiques, architectural details, and old books.

LILI GOLDBERG

When was your home built?

LG: The original part of the house was built in 1795.

What is its history?

LG: An enterprising gentleman purchased the entire village in the late eighteenth century, and our house was amongst these.

When did it become yours?

LG: We purchased the house in 2006.

What drew you to your home? What do you love most about it?

LG: What drew me to the home was the look of the village (very New England) and the nicest row of houses in the Berkshires. Love the porch, especially in the summer and fall.

How have you put your mark on it?

LG: We have put our mark on it by introducing our English and French antiques.

Where do you look for decor inspiration?

LG: I definitely look to England and France for decor inspiration, though I admit that if I could afford it, I would own more eighteenth-century American objects, furniture, and paintings.

What are your favorite shops or sources for furnishings? For decorative objects? For art?

LG: My favorite shops in the area are Cabbages & Roses and Susan Silver Antiques, both in Sheffield, Massachusetts. These shops are great for paintings, furniture, and decorative objects as well.

Do you consider plants and flowers decorative objects?

LG: I definitely consider flowers and plants as decorative objects—I have my home full of fresh flowers every week. I grow amaryllis and always have at least two beautiful orchids at all times. One of my greatest regrets moving from Paris were the flower shops there—I am consoled by the fact that the local farmers' markets have wonderful flowers from May until late October.

How do you decide where to place your decorative objects?

LG: I always move objects around, but I know I have a talent for "placing objects," as I've been told several times by friends.

How have you acquired your decorative objects and furnishings?

LG: Mainly in France and London, buying what I love and then placing it in my home. I seldom consider size, but just go ahead and buy and then decide where to place the item.

Do you have any favorite pieces?

LG: I have many favorite pieces as any collector would tell you, but just to name a few: two eighteenth-century paintings of ladies, an eighteenth-century blue urn, and my collection of Chinese eighteenth- and nineteenth-century blue-and-white porcelain.

What is your favorite place to spend time in your home, and what do you do there?

LG: Strangely enough, even though the living room is so peaceful and beautiful, we spend all of our time in the library for the simple reason that the television is there (never had a TV in any of our previous living rooms), as well as a fabulous fireplace, which we use on a daily basis at night from October right until May.

How would you describe the French approach to the details of a home?

LG: The French approach is very simple indeed! Bring in beauty through the past, meaning with antiques, paintings, flowers, objets d'art, and, above all, do not worry about scratches, missing pieces, or damaged furniture or objects—the older, the better, and they should look as such. Mixing styles is one of the oldest and wisest rules the French apply, I think. In short, a home should be comfortable and filled with beautiful things you enjoy in your everyday life! That's the French savoir faire!

Fresh, green plants in a porous stone urn and stand look especially lively compared with the animal-horn trophy, papier-mâché deer head, and eighteenth-century painting of a dog. Natural things always add fresh and welcome texture.

PRECEDING SPREAD An antique baker's table is loaded with treasures, including vintage books, new and old stone pieces, and mounted birds. The eighteenth-century French mirror has a mottled surface similar to the other unique finds.

OPPOSITE Beside a doorway trimmed with carved moldings, colorful birds perch atop piles of beautiful volumes; a leafy branch, an eighteenth-century French painting, and a trophy of antlers fill the wall. A colorful rug connects the pale-grey room with the brightly painted foyer.

STRUCTURE
LA STRUCTURE

French homes often have spectacular structure. Gothic and classical influences make for buildings with very good bones. High ceilings, often with molding, paneled walls, oval and round rooms, towering French windows, and beautiful brass hardware combine in fantastic ways; together these elements form the foundation for all other decor. But, even though the architecture is difficult to replicate, there are elements that can be incorporated into any home. Moldings can be purchased at a local hardware store. Mantelpieces and hardware can be found at flea markets or antiques shops. Floor-to-ceiling drapes offer the illusion that the windows they adorn are of the same dimensions. Structure is about architecture and hardware, but it's also about shape and form. In that way, furniture, accents, and art can also be used to create structure, elevate existing architecture, manipulate space, and give your home any look you desire.

ABOVE The nineteenth-century home's paneled walls and chimneypiece are topped with egg-and-dart, *raies de cœur,* and acanthus-leaf moldings. The panels' unexpected colors give added definition to the carved trims.

BELOW The Arc de Triomphe is one of the most remarkable monuments in Paris, commissioned by Napoléon Bonaparte to commemorate his empire. Its form shows how impactful a combination of straight and curved lines can be, whether on an enormous stone monument or in the structure, furnishings, and accents of your home.

OPPOSITE In a clever use of space, a powder room is tucked beneath a stairwell; the entry boasts beautiful chrome hardware.

PRECEDING SPREAD The layout of this home allows a clear view from the living room through the dining room and into the kitchen when the interior doors are open. This is a very typical and much admired layout in a Parisian flat.

HAUTE HEARTHS

THOUGH IT'S BEEN some time since French homes relied on the fireplace for heat, the importance of hearths and, more to the point, the mantelpieces around them, has not diminished. In a home of a certain age, the design of the mantel will indicate the period in which the building was constructed, and will tie in with all the other architectural elements. Because life so often revolved around the hearth, it was decorated in a way befitting the focal point of a home. Mantelshelves became an opportunity to display prized items, and the wall space above them was often paneled or decorated with art or ornate mirrors. The wonderful thing about mantels is that they can be added to homes with no fireplaces at all or upgraded in homes with modest fireplaces. Traditionally, people avoided hanging paintings above mantels for fear the soot from the fireplace would damage the art, hence the mirrors instead, but there are no hard-and-fast rules. You'll find even televisions above fireplaces, depending on the taste of the homeowner. Custom-made, built with a DIY kit, or purchased new from a hardware store or secondhand from an architectural-salvage or antiques shop, mantels are sure to add charm to your home.

The fireplace in this bedroom boasts a chic assemblage of an antique French toy horse, design tomes, and a scattering of artworks, all crowned with an abstract painting by Marco Croce. The pieces, their colors, and the asymmetrical clustering of objects on the mantel make the scene a delight for the eye.

OPPOSITE The black-and-white nineteenth-century mantel and a contemporary painting by Ruben Alterio are drawn together by the menagerie scattered between them. Black candles in a seashell holder reminiscent of J. C. Moreux and sleek contemporary candlesticks mix with African artifacts, a glossy black vase of fresh flowers, and spiny pieces of coral.

In a home with ornate
architectural elements,
experiment with simplicity
in furniture and decor.

ABOVE A skylight welcomes sunshine into an office, where an oak-veneered panel above the desk lets the homeowner display her current image inspirations. The contrast between the exposed wooden beams, the lightweight desk, the heavy oak chair, and airy skylight creates a memorable look. The built-in desk and cabinetry allow for an excellent use of space and make a cozy nook for work.

BELOW The blond Sycamore-wood paneling and exposed stairway are suggestive of Scandinavian-modern design. This is a prime example of the French practice of blending old and new architecture to create a cohesive home; once an old factory, this is now a home with many one-of-a-kind features.

OPPOSITE The height of the floor-to-ceiling windows is enhanced by the Le Corbusier glass dining table, set with Arne Jacobsen chairs, and antique lights hung as pendants from the ceiling.

PRECEDING SPREAD, LEFT The contemporary furnishings look striking in a room with ornate classical moldings and herringbone floors; the contrasting forms illustrate how well styles from different periods can work together.

PRECEDING SPREAD, RIGHT Glass panels and doors were built into an arched doorway in a centuries-old home to highlight the form of the entrance and allow in light. Natural-stone floors continue to the courtyard for a seamless look.

seek out surprising structural elements to add architectural appeal and a sense of ceremony to your interiors.

RESCUED RELICS

HISTORIC REFERENCES are inherent in the style seen in French homes, and very often, just as important as antique furnishings are the bones of the place—paneled walls capped by decorative moldings, old wooden doors, marble mantels, and timeworn floors. If you admire the look of those elements but find your home lacking in original eighteenth-century structural details, seek out architectural-salvage shops in your area or online. The entrepreneurs behind these operations make a practice of rescuing precious period details from buildings marked for demolition or renovation, such as churches, schools, theaters, homes, hotels, and even factories. As a result, their shops and warehouses become treasure troves of architecture and design elements, and a great place for homeowners and designers to source unique pieces.

Visit one of these salvage shops in person or peruse their selection online and you may find stained-glass windows, exterior and interior doors, mantelpieces made from stone and wood, and formerly weight-bearing columns and corbels that may be used to add decorative interest to your home. If you're looking for lighting, you may find chandeliers and sconces of all styles alongside industrial fixtures and lamps. Salvage shops also often stock wooden planks, tiles, and stones that allow even newly installed floors to look elegantly aged, and wrought-iron gates and balcony railings that can be repurposed as one-of-a-kind room dividers in your home. Many of these shops even supplement their architectural offerings with antique and vintage furnishings and decorative accessories, making them even more enticing as shopping destinations.

Here are some noteworthy salvage shops and showrooms in the United States:

Old Portland Hardware and Architectural
4035 SE Division Street
Portland, OR 97202

Salvage One
1840 West Hubbard Street
Chicago, IL 60622

Sarasota Architectural Salvage
1093 Central Avenue
Sarasota, FL 34236

Silver Fox Salvage
20 Learned Street
Albany, NY 12207
and
1060 E. Cesar E. Chavez Avenue
Los Angeles, CA 90033

Urban Archaeology
143 Franklin Street
New York, NY 10013
and
239 East 58th Street
New York, NY 10022
and
2231 Montauk Highway
Bridgehampton, NY 11932
and
The Merchandise Mart
222 Merchandise Mart Plaza
Suite 108
Chicago, IL 60654

OPPOSITE An iron garden gate is repurposed as a door, opening into the petite kitchen, creating a dramatic boundary between the workspace and the dining room.

PERFECT PULLS, KNOBS, AND LEVERS

Door and cabinet hardware can instantly elevate your home's decor. They can also introduce or enhance period details in your home's structure or furnishings. In the same way that a fresh coat of paint makes something old look new, so, too, are new pulls, knobs, and levers simple additions that make a major impact. Depending on the style and finish, they may add a bit of glimmer, history, or an architectural or sculptural note to your decor.

The variety in door and cabinet hardware is amazing, so a thorough search is almost certain to yield the perfect style for your home. There are three main points to consider in selecting your knobs, pulls, and levers: aesthetics, maintenance, and cost. First think about the look you're after and use that to narrow down your options. Are you looking for pieces with a certain period appeal, like neoclassical, art deco, or midcentury modern? Try searching within those parameters and see what you find.

Along with the style, you'll have to think about material and finish. Most door and cabinet hardware is made of metal, glass, or natural stone. In surveying the metal varieties, you'll find that they are often made of one kind, say copper, brass, or stainless steel, but they might have a completely different finish, like chrome, nickel, or even gold plate. As you're considering the different metal finishes, or other materials like glass or natural stone for your hardware, be sure to inquire about the recommended maintenance, as some require frequent polishing and others, very gentle cleaning to retain their beauty. Here are some examples:

1. ORNATE

2. ORNATE 3. ORNATE

4. CLASSIC 5. ORNATE

6. MODERN 7. MODERN

8. MODERN

9. MODERN 10. CLASSIC

11. MODERN 12. CLASSIC

13. MODERN 14. ORNATE

15. MODERN

BRASS requires regular polishing; left alone, it will tarnish. Some people like a bit of tarnish, as they consider it part of the attractive patina of brass. For those who prefer to spend less time polishing, there are protective coatings that may be applied to brass to prevent it from tarnishing and aging. The coating itself is a bit delicate, however, requiring gentle cleaning with a soft cloth and soapy water.

BRONZE needs little polishing, but the kind of care required depends on the type of bronze finish and the desired look. Generally, age and wear contribute to an attractive patina over time.

NICKEL is a very versatile and relatively low-maintenance metal. It is available in a variety of looks; some are shiny like chrome, others are more matte. The less reflective the finish, the fewer fingerprints, watermarks, and other signs of daily use that will show.

CHROME is a brilliant, tarnish-resistant finish, but its high shine requires frequent cleaning.

STAINLESS STEEL will not tarnish, rust, or corrode, but may dull slightly over time.

NATURAL STONE boasts long-lasting beauty that will not fade. If the stone is highly polished, it will need regular cleaning to remove fingerprints and handprints.

GLASS OR PORCELAIN requires gentle cleaning, especially when painted. Abrasive cleaners or sponges should be avoided.

GOLD OR SILVER PLATE should be cleaned with a soft rag in warm soapy water, so as not to scratch the finish. Silver plate may tarnish over time, though gold will not, but to maintain shine, either finish may be polished with a gold- or silver-polishing cloth, and tarnish remover may be used as necessary.

The design itself will also impact the required maintenance: the more intricate it is, the more cleaning it will need. In some cases a soft toothbrush may be used along with a soft rag to gently remove any dirt or oils from the finer details of the hardware.

The cost of hardware is determined by the value of the materials, the finish, and the craftsmanship. Because prices for pulls, knobs, and levers vary widely, it's best to determine your ideal budget for hardware, and keep in mind how many cabinets, drawers, or doors you need to outfit. Consider mixing complementary styles with a uniting feature (finish, for example). This can also help to stretch your budget: consider employing the dearer pieces in a limited way to create a focal point—maybe on the cabinets above your stove or sink—and choose complementary but more affordable ones for the rest of the drawers and cabinets. Best of all, a combination of styles will create a look that is unique to your home alone.

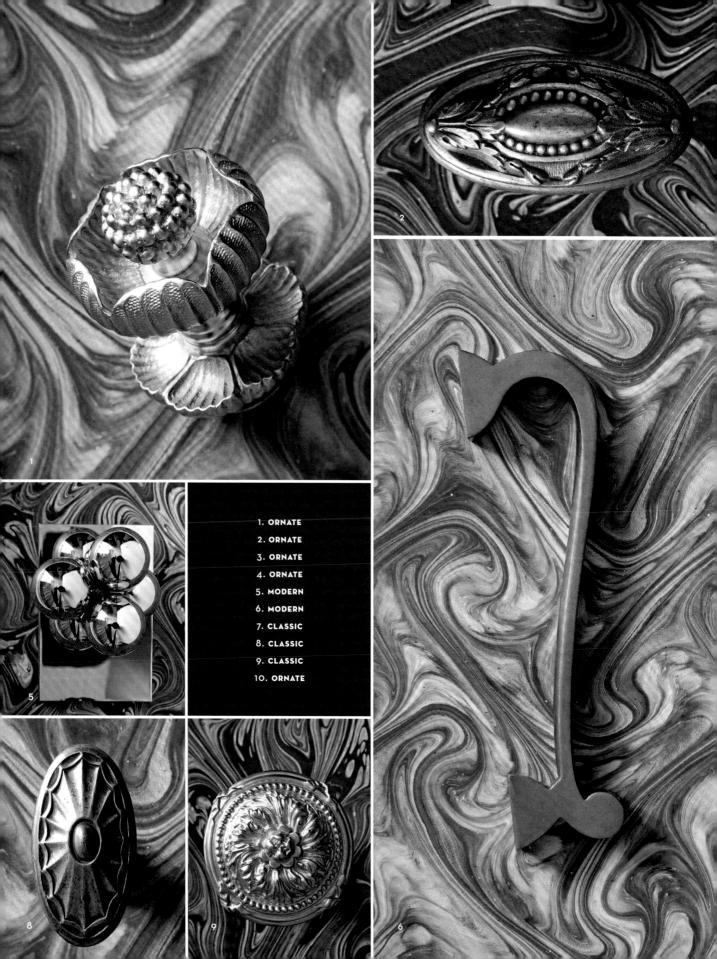

1. ORNATE

2. ORNATE

3. ORNATE

4. ORNATE

5. MODERN

6. MODERN

7. CLASSIC

8. CLASSIC

9. CLASSIC

10. ORNATE

FANTASTIC FRENCH WINDOWS AND DOORS

WINDOWS AND DOORS are among the most noteworthy architectural elements of French homes. Holdovers from the Gothic period include small windows with their diamond-shaped leaded-glass panes, and robust, wide-plank, board-and-batten doors. Later, classically influenced building styles introduced the now-iconic "French" paired casement windows extending all the way to the floor, and the paneled double doors with similar dimensions used in interiors. Short of renovating your home to add these features, there are a few ways you can mimic them:

WINDOWS

Give any small windows in your home the Gothic treatment with self-adhesive lead strips, applied in the diamond pattern of the period.

Create the illusion of tall French windows with dramatic, floor-to-ceiling, double-panel draperies. Hang sheers to let in light but disguise the standard windows behind them. Then add an outer layer of draperies of a more substantial fabric, which can be held open with tiebacks, exposing the sheers.

DOORS

Seek out Gothic-style doors at flea markets or antiques stores. Know the dimensions you need, but remember that doors can be shaved to better fit a doorway.

Add detail to your existing doors with carved-wood moldings or trompe l'oeil paint.

Install double doors—even narrow ones—in interior doorways. You may also use a pair of paneled shutters to replicate the look of French doors.

French doors open out to wrought-iron railings and a mansard roof beyond, a beloved view of Paris.

OPPOSITE Glass-and-iron doors show the brilliance of the brief art deco period in Paris. The pattern on the door can be re-created in your home with reclaimed wrought iron, self-adhesive lead strips, or even paint.

Get wild. Choose a
statement piece, like an
outré armchair, and build a
room around it, balancing
its boldness with other
more subtle elements.

This living room's Prelle silk-velvet curtains highlight the ceiling-height, double-pane windows that France is so known for. The back-to-back custom sofas designed by Robert Couturier and covered in yellow Fortuny fabric split the room into two cozy sitting areas, while the two single-panel, full-length drapes frame the space and make it feel unified.

PRECEDING SPREAD Classical moldings, floor-to-ceiling draperies, and stand-out furnishings—including an armchair with animal-horn and -hide details, an eighteenth-century Chinese calamander tabletop on a nineteenth-century gilt-iron base, and an Asian opium stool dating from 1900—come together to create a remarkable room. Even amid such bold furnishings and decoration, the dramatic bones of the room itself draw notice.

Make a large living room more intimate by arranging furniture into smaller, more inviting sections.

MAGNIFICENT MANSARDS

THE MANSARD ROOF, with its hipped shapes and dormer windows, can be found in many cities around the world, but the one it's most often associated with is Paris. Characterized by having two slopes on all sides, with the lower slope steeper than the upper one, and punctuated with windows, the style was named for seventeenth-century architect François Mansart, who was not its originator, but who used it frequently in his designs.

The mansard's heyday came more than a hundred years later, when Baron Georges-Eugène Haussmann was charged by Napoléon III to reengineer the city of Paris, which had seen a population explosion that was choking its medieval streets and overcrowding its buildings. Among the notable features of Haussmann's urban planning, and the resulting Napoléon III style, was the resurgence of the mansard roof, which helped achieve the goal of easing overcrowding by raising the ceiling on the top floor of the building, creating habitable attic apartments.

Perhaps it's because of Paris and its mansard roofs that a room with a slanted ceiling and dormer windows evokes a sense of romance. Maybe it inspires thoughts of the artists, writers, and lovers who may have occupied the attic flats beneath those Parisian mansards. Or perhaps the fascination is purely architectural, rooted in the dramatic angles resulting from the slanted ceilings and dormers. Either way, these rooms present excellent opportunities for statement-making decorating and some practical options, too:

TAKE A BOLD APPROACH TO SURFACES
Make the most of the room's unique dimensions by covering the slanted ceiling with a stand-out color or wallpaper and leaving the walls within the dormer white. It creates a graphic look and also makes the most of the light coming through the window.

TREAT THE CEILING LIKE A WALL
Adorn the angled surface with artwork, just as you would a vertical wall. To keep the frames in place, purchase security hangers from the hardware store, which typically include anchors, t-screws, and brackets, as well as a wrench to turn the t-screws. The brackets should be affixed to the top and bottom of each frame; the anchor and t-screw go into the wall, and the wrench is used to tighten the t-screw into the bracket, keeping the frame locked into place.

CHOOSE DRAMATIC DRAPERIES
Consider a cornice, roman shades, or a window treatment of your choice that is hung high above the window within the dormer, maximizing the appearance of the window and the overall sense of space in the room.

CREATE A SPACIOUS *SALLE DE BAIN*
Consider using the space as a bathroom. A shower or tub built into a dormer or under an angled ceiling can still feel spacious, despite the limited standing room.

SNEAK IN STORAGE
If the point at which the slanted ceiling meets the vertical wall is too low to accommodate furniture, add built-in shelves or cabinetry to house linens, clothing, shoes, or books.

Make the most of a space inside a dormer window. Add an upholstered bench or chair to create a reading nook or a tub so you can take baths while gazing outside.

OPPOSITE Topped by identical French lamps from the 1960s, dressers of different heights flank the window and an upholstered bench from 1940s France. The arrangement of the pieces makes the room look both taller and wider.

The books, vases, and lamp on this dresser strike a perfect visual balance, which is key when creating structure and form within a home. The photos stuck into the mirror's gilt frame and necklaces draped on the lamp shade personalize the look.

ABOVE A neon pharmacy sign is embellished with loops of wrought iron to match the charm of its picturesque location; structural details like these may be found in flea markets or salvage shops and integrated into your home as art.

BELOW Cobblestones, topiaries and other plants, and colorful awnings make up the Parisian streetscape. Consider mimicking the pattern of the stone streets in the floor of your bathroom and shower.

OPPOSITE The kitchen table is a bar-height custom-made oak-and-limestone piece of the homeowner Jean-Louis Deniot's design, set with chairs from Williams-Sonoma Home. The floor is covered in traditional French black-and-white cement tiles. The table and 1880s French Épis de Blé chandeliers create a symmetrical effect.

Eschew the
kitchen island for
a counter-height
kitchen table. Use it
as a work surface
when needed, and
as a casual but
elegant dining setup
at other times.

ABOVE Moldings dating back to 1860 reflect the Second Empire architectural style. Gilt paint enhances the ornateness of a plaster cornice at the corner and trophy detail in the panels.

BELOW Neutral colors and lustrous metallics come together in this arrangement of objects and collector's pieces. A metal garden table found at a French flea market is repurposed as an elegant side table and topped with an Axis Mundi table lamp from Ochre and vintage dough bowls, which, taken out of the kitchen, look more sculptural than functional. An abstract painting by Jeri Ledbetter hangs on the wall.

OPPOSITE The home's high ceilings and small windows hint at its age: both features were common in the Gothic period. Windows were small both for security and because glass was rare and available only in small panes.

WELL MOLDED

The French have been adorning their walls since the Middle Ages, when paneling, friezes, and murals depicting religious themes first appeared. The Renaissance introduced more ornate stucco and wood carvings (or *boiserie*) of medallions, cornucopias, urns, swags of fruit, garlands, and plant, animal, and human forms. These ornamental wall treatments would evolve in the following centuries, but the themes would remain largely the same, leaning heavily on classical design.

Today, molding is still used, both as a reference to earlier periods in design and also for a practical reason: to protect the walls and to disguise unsightly seams. The most common types of molding are crown molding and baseboards. These pieces line the ceiling and floor, respectively, to create clean lines between them and the wall treatment. Baseboards also protect walls from possible damage due to cleaning with brooms, vacuums, and mops. Chair rails are another protective molding, placed at the point where chair backs might bang into the wall. The chair rail provides a barrier for easily dented plaster, Sheetrock, or drywall.

Those purposeful elements became more and more embellished over time. In Renaissance-style wall moldings that run along the ceiling, there are three horizontal layers: (1) the architrave, the lowest of the three, which supports (2) the frieze, or decorative middle section, which in turn is topped with (3) the cornice, the piece closest to the ceiling. Currently, there are decorative moldings available in many styles to suit any decor, whether Old World, traditional, or contemporary. Moldings may be clean and streamlined, or intricately carved with craftsmanship that hearkens back to the work of Renaissance artisans. Consider them puzzle pieces and experiment with different combinations to come up with the look that's perfect for your home. Customize moldings further by choosing a finish. They may be stained and varnished to highlight the grain of the wood, or painted white, an accent color, or the same color as the walls, so they can stand out or blend in as much as you like.

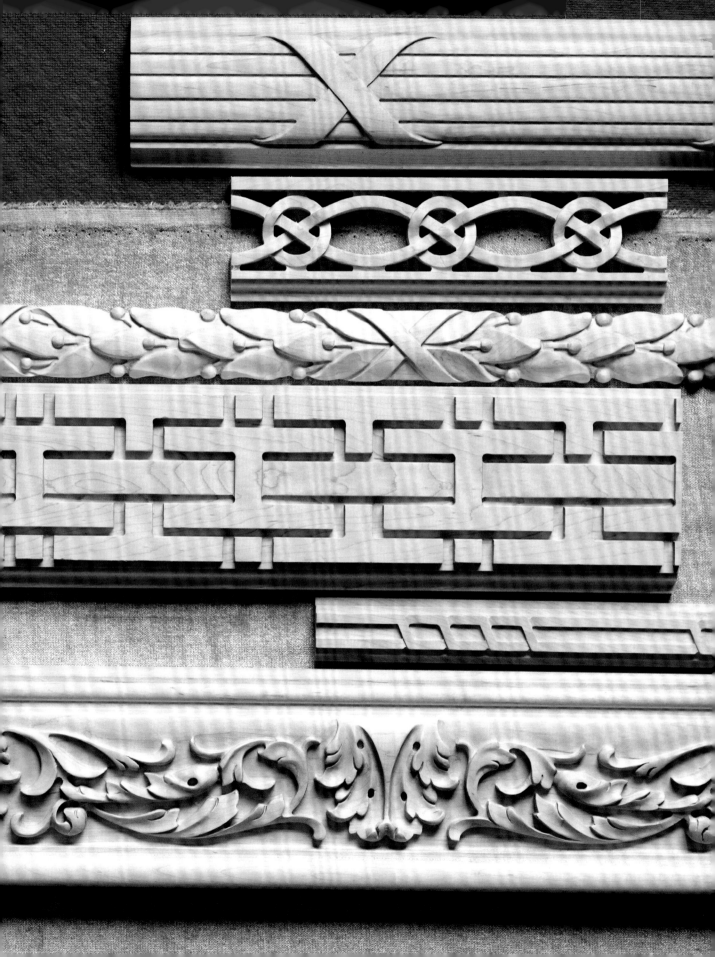

2

3

4

10

11

12

16

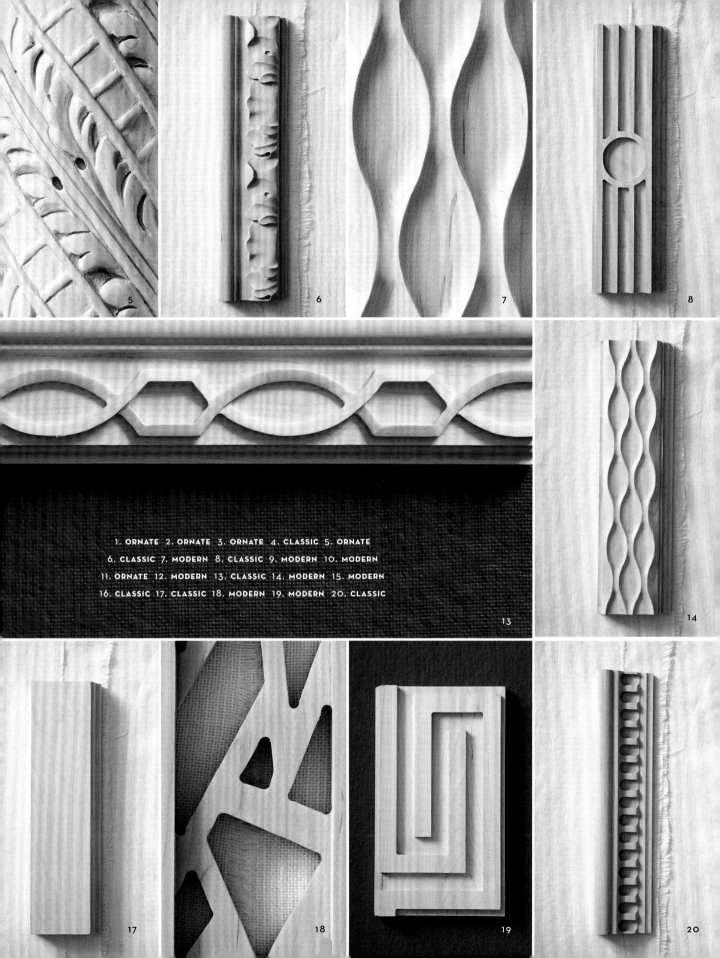

1. **ORNATE** 2. **ORNATE** 3. **ORNATE** 4. **CLASSIC** 5. **ORNATE**
6. **CLASSIC** 7. **MODERN** 8. **CLASSIC** 9. **MODERN** 10. **MODERN**
11. **ORNATE** 12. **MODERN** 13. **CLASSIC** 14. **MODERN** 15. **MODERN**
16. **CLASSIC** 17. **CLASSIC** 18. **MODERN** 19. **MODERN** 20. **CLASSIC**

1. CLASSIC

2. ORNATE 3. ORNATE

4. MODERN 5. ORNATE

6. MODERN 7. MODERN

8. CLASSIC

9. CLASSIC 10. CLASSIC

11. MODERN 12. CLASSIC

13. CLASSIC 14. MODERN

15. MODERN

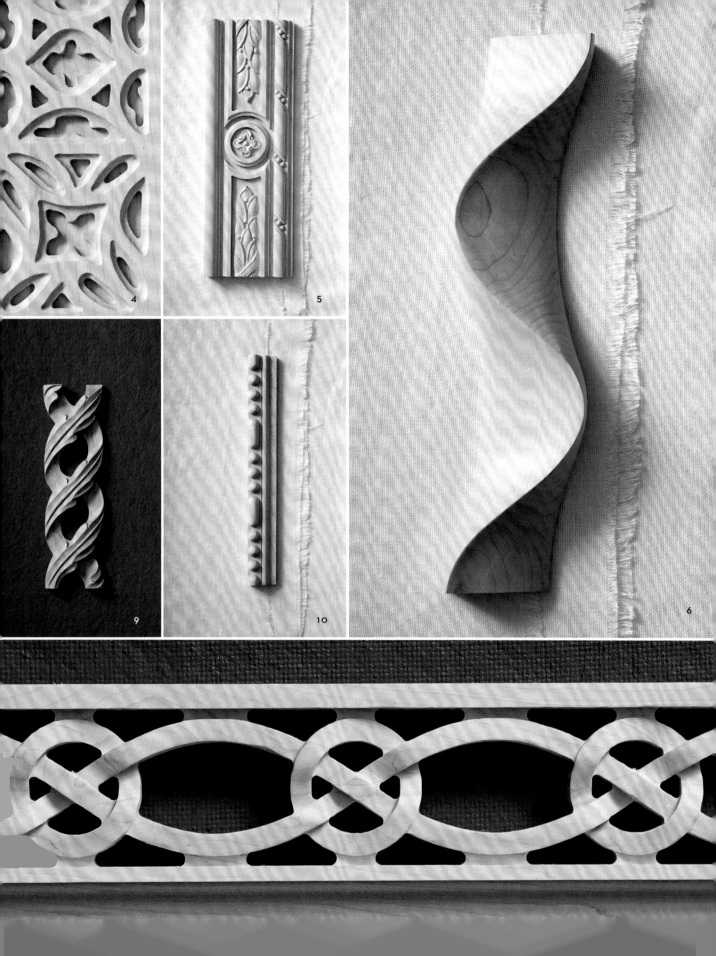

Coordinated doesn't necessarily mean dull. If you can't resist getting a little matchy-matchy, take it to the extreme and you'll still achieve an unexpected and dynamic look.

JEAN-LOUIS DENIOT

When was your home built?

JLD: The center of the house was built in 1810, and the wings of the house came later, in the 1880s.

What is its history?

JLD: Before the wings and the "fancy looking" embellishments, the house belonged to a farmer who used to own a large amount of land in the area. As he got richer, he decided to turn his farmhouse into a *manoir.*

When did it become yours?

JLD: I found it over ten years ago. There was only one bathroom for the entire 7,500-square-foot house! After all the improvements, there are now seven bathrooms!

What drew you to your home? What do you love most about it?

JLD: I loved the architecture, as it is grand and simple at the same time. The fifteen acres of land, which include three-hundred-year-old trees and natural-spring rivers, make it very special, particularly during the spring, summer, and autumn. I was also attracted to the fact that it was only ten miles away from Charles de Gaulle airport and thirty miles from Paris.

How have you put your mark on it?

JLD: I stripped it all the way down and tried to change all the existing finishes as it was really gloomy, like a Victor Hugo house. I wanted a fresh, inviting, playful, comfortable, and stylish house!

Where do you look for decor inspiration?

JLD: Inspiration comes from my dreams. I get inspired by pieces I buy and then I build a decor around them. I wanted to respect the formality of the grand living room, but with added comfort and with a little less "Louis"! All the bedrooms have a theme and style so as to optimize my guests' stay, and also so that with each visit, they have a different experience.

What are your favorite shops or sources for furnishings?

JLD: I shop at the Porte de Clignancourt and Porte de Vanves flea markets and also get a lot of pieces from Onsite Antiques gallery, at 58 rue de l'Université in Paris. I buy in Belgium, Denmark, and London, to name a few. I buy everything everywhere! There are no pieces that can escape me.

For decorative objects?

JLD: The same sources. I've found pieces in Monaco, in Los Angeles, at yard sales in New York. Everywhere.

For art?

JLD: For country houses, I most often buy prints or portraits. I prefer a good eighteenth-century print rather than a mediocre nineteenth-century painting. Portraits from all periods are fun; it's like adding new members of family.

What are your favorite structural details—doors, windows, moldings—in your home?

JLD: I really like the main living room and the grey vestibule as they are very Louis XVI. It's very architectural and more of a pure style, whereas in many of the other rooms the style is more Napoléon III.

How have you used paint to highlight or conceal the structural details of your home?

JLD: I play with three or four different tones on paneling, to highlight the moldings and the decorative plaster motifs, and to give a better sense of rhythm and volume. In the living room, I used the landscape colors as the main inspiration for the paneling palette as the room features a lot of landscape views.

Where have you introduced contemporary features into the structure of your home, and what inspired you?

JLD: When remodeling, I always like to create my own version of the history of the building so that the place is not a reproduction. I do not like period rooms; I prefer my own interpretation. The design should suit the building as well as incorporate the look and lifestyle of the twenty-first century.

How does the period of your home impact your choice of furnishings?

JLD: The period of the house did not really impact my choice of furnishings. I just tried to keep everything low key, as the worst thing would have been to decorate it as a pretentious castle wannabe! The last thing I wanted was a house with a social complex. It is a cool, happy house with friends always around—sipping wine, eating, and dancing at all times of the day.

How have you placed furnishings within your home to highlight interesting structural details?

JLD: They are placed in a quite formal way, so as to respect symmetry and balance. I like a room to have a certain theatricality when you come and sit in it. I love drama, what can I say? I always have in mind the way Louis XIV, Louis XV, or Louis XVI used to place furniture, and I cannot help it. If it worked at the time, then it should still work now.

How have you used furnishings to create unique spaces within your home?

JLD: I buy only one or two good pieces for each room; the rest are fillers. For example, I purchased a Maison Jansen coffee table, dining table, side table, and desk. I also purchased some great antiques from England and France to create a focal point and a sense of quality. What makes it look low-key is that everything else is just stuff from attics!

Can you tell us more about the floors in your home?

JLD: There is terrazzo flooring in the entry hall, which is not my favorite, but it was already there. There is also a dark chocolate-brown herringbone wooden floor. I installed limestone in the circulation areas such as the hallways, black and beige *carreaux de ciment* tiling in the kitchen in reference to French brasseries, marble in all the bathrooms, and wall-to-wall sisal in the master apartment to maximize the coziness and soundproofing.

What is your favorite place to spend time in your home, and what do you do there?

JLD: Probably the master apartment. The suite is about 1,300 square feet and is comprised of a sitting room with bookcases and a fireplace, a very large bathroom and dressing area, and a large bedroom with a fireplace and a king-sized bed! There is also a 300-square-foot terrace overlooking the garden.

How would you describe the French approach to the details of a home?

JLD: I do French as I do not know how to do otherwise. In any country where I work, I always bring a touch of French flair no matter what. This house was so French to start with that I actually made it less so! I mixed twenty-first-century living with international comfort and a fun, eclectic palette and style.

Enhance your ceiling. Add decorative moldings, or replicate them with paint or stencils to create a ceiling medallion.

ABOVE A 1940s Maison Baguès chandelier with crystal beads hangs from a ceiling adorned with a plaster-leaf detail.

BELOW The house is a quintessential French château, with the classic French windows and dormers on the slate roof. The structure of the exterior hints at the rooms inside.

PRECEDING SPREAD A Napoléon III–style slipper chair is covered in a Pierre Frey toile fabric; the same pattern is used in the window treatments and on the walls in a very clever application. The repeated motif contributes visual texture to the room.

TEXTURE
LA TEXTURE

Just as French women dress in a manner that appears effortless and instinctive, so too do the French combine textures in their homes. Plush and coarse, glossy and matte elements come together to add richness, sensuousness, and sophistication to a space. Antiqued mirrors create imperfect reflections; velvet sumptuously covers chairs, sofas, and windows; gauzy sheers hang over bathtubs; and decorative pillows and blankets add softness. Texture creates ease within interiors: no matter how fine or formal the interior, comfort is never sacrificed for style. Every room is designed to look and feel inviting, to encourage lingering over dinner, conversations that continue late into the night, or long, quiet hours spent in the company of one's thoughts.

PRECEDING SPREAD A variety of black pieces with different finishes come together on and below a 1940s Italian console table. The Burmese temple box and nineteenth-century Chinese jar are glossy, while the linen shade on top of the silver English lamp and the black linen-bound books are matte. The branches above and the leaves below add more textures.

ABOVE A chevron hardwood floor is the foundation for the kitchen, where an enameled-iron Aga range is topped by a custom-made glass hood of the homeowner's design. Metallic decorative accessories modeled on kitchen utensils hang from the hood. Metal shelving provides storage and a vintage post office bureau acts as the kitchen table. The contrasting textures of the metal, glass, and wood add to the beauty of the space.

OPPOSITE The kitchen mixes light and dark, glossy and matte. Beech-and-aluminum chairs by Antonio Citterio pull up to an Ikea table, topped with an English tea set that adds a note of history. The cabinetry is finished in black stain with frosted-glass fronts and glazed-lava countertops.

Combine different finishes in a room to create distinctive spaces within it.

WONDERFUL WOOD FINISHES

HARDWOOD FLOORS are prized in French homes. They are left exposed as much as possible, and when they're covered, it's most likely with a beautiful rug, rather than with wall-to-wall carpeting. Many styles of wood floors exist in France, with variations like herringbone, chevron, and wide plank, but any wood floor can be refinished in a way that evokes the French style.

STAIN There are dozens of shades available for wood stains, but the most authentically French colors tend to be on the light side, with honey and light chocolate-brown shades being the most popular.

URETHANE FLOOR FINISH Stained floors can be sealed with a urethane top coat for protection and to achieve a glossy finish, though matte and satin finishes are also available.

EUROPEAN OIL FINISH This technique is used to add a protective surface to wood floors that has a more natural look. The flat sheen it produces wears well and in fact looks better with time and, unlike urethane floors, may never need to be refinished if cared for properly.

PAINT Applied properly, in thin layers, paint can both transform the look of a hardwood floor and highlight its texture. Floors can be painted one solid color or in a pattern, which may be simple and geometric or highly detailed, like a trompe l'oeil Oriental-rug motif.

The scratches and scuffs in the black stain of the herringbone floors in this nineteenth-century home add to their charm. Many hours of late-night dancing contributed to the one-of-a-kind patina.

OPPOSITE Bridge chairs from 1940s France, reupholstered in vintage Chanel bouclé fabric, are set around a black Saarinen table. The walls are adorned with art, including Christopher Draghi photos of the Eiffel Tower.

Choose high-contrast materials. A high-gloss dining table looks refined and masculine with chairs covered in toothy tweed.

The cool blues and greys of the bathroom's slate floor and cast-iron tub get a bit of sparkle courtesy of the glossy ceramic of the tub's lining and the Venetian-glass mirror.

OPPOSITE In front of the fireplace, the furnishings are sleek, but the different textures make the room look rich. The mercury-glass mirror reflects the natural light in the room, while the matte black mantel absorbs it; in an eccentric touch, leather-bound books fill the fireplace, adding a splash of color.

SOFT SOPHISTICATION

THROW BLANKETS and pillows are a special kind of decor because they add both comfort and polish. A room may have all the necessary pieces of furniture, but it's the blanket draped at the foot of the bed or the plush pillows added to a sofa that finish the look. And because these items are soft by definition, they make a sophisticated space look more inviting, too.

Given the emphasis on comfort in French homes, it's no wonder that throw blankets and pillows are used so well in them. Soft goods may add a pop of color, like an orange blanket in a room of muted blues and greys, or a pillow with a vibrant print on a solid-color sofa. They're also statement making when they match the color of their background but have a contrasting texture, like a white mohair blanket on a white cotton sofa, a tan cashmere blanket on a linen sofa of the same color, or a deep-green velvet pillow on a similarly hued damask chair.

OPPOSITE Layers of texture make this bed look so inviting and cozy, it's hard to resist climbing in: the headboard is upholstered in grey flannel; the crisp white sheets and duvet are topped with an Hermès blanket. A Lucite lamp and a nineteenth-century English carafe filled with flowers top the horn-and-chrome Italian side table.

The animal-fur–covered bed is the centerpiece of an exposed-brick bedroom. A nineteenth-century Oriental rug is layered on top of a neutral carpet. The antiqued bedside lamps complement the finish on the bricks, while the lacquered orange midcentury-modern French bureau adds vibrant color and a contrasting texture to the room.

When upholstering or reupholstering, choose the best fabric in your budget and don't be afraid of color or pattern.

A linen sofa topped with French accent pillows, a dark-leather cube, French leather club chairs, and a faded blue-and-cream rug create an invitingly cozy look.

PRECEDING SPREAD, LEFT A custom sofa designed by Robert Couturier is beautifully upholstered in red silk velvet by Prelle. Every pleat and crease in the velvet highlights its luxurious texture. A pillow in embroidered Chelsea Editions fabric renders the color of the sofa even more vivid.

PRECEDING SPREAD, RIGHT Original wrought-iron and brass hardware around the window is paired with incredibly lush silk-velvet drapes with ribbon trim.

TEXTILE SENSATION

The rich, multilayered textures in French homes are attributable in great part to the use of fabrics. Varying weights and weaves enhance a room's beauty and comfort. Searching for textiles for your home is a bit like shopping for clothes. Of course, when choosing fabrics to use in your home, the stakes are higher because you may live with your fabrics, unlike an item of clothing, every day for years. That means you need to find a look that appeals to you in the moment but that will also stand the test of time, and you need that fabric to be durable enough for the purpose you have in mind. Is it perfect for your living-room sofa, or would it be better for the seats of your dining chairs? Would it look great on a tufted ottoman, or hung from a window as roman shades?

The ease of French style would suggest that you should simply find a fabric you love and use it wherever it's most pleasing to you. But if you want to combine that approach with a bit of practical knowledge, you might consider a textile's inherent strength, its weave—which means how warp (vertical threads) meets weft (the horizontal fibers threaded through the warp)—the way it holds dye, and its breathability. Here are some notes to help guide choice of fabrics:

SILK is a delicate fabric in that it is difficult to clean, and even water may leave a stain. Though there are upholstery-weight varieties, silk should still be used thoughtfully. If you find a delicate silk that you love, consider using it as an accent— perhaps on the skirt of a chair, on the back of a sofa, to cover buttons, or to make piping or trim—or for window treatments. In any application, it is always advisable to knit-back silk, which involves adhering cotton or a similar fabric to the back of the silk to give it added strength. Because silk is susceptible to sun damage (referred to as sun rot), silk window treatments should also be interlined, adding an extra layer of protection on the side facing the sun.

COTTON is the most popular fabric used in upholstery. Cotton fiber is strong and durable, and can be made into many different styles of textiles, from casual to formal. In addition to being naturally soft to the touch, it is also extremely breathable, making it a very comfortable fabric for seat furniture. Finally, cotton absorbs

LINEN, like cotton, is a plant-based fabric that boasts strength and breathability. Linen has an appealing texture, whether the fabric is very fine or very hardy, but all linen wrinkles; for many people, that is part of its charm. It is versatile like cotton, too, so if wrinkles can be tolerated, linen can be used well throughout the home. If the linen you love most is a very fine one, it can be knit-backed, just like silk, for added strength.

WOOL is a long-lasting, very strong natural fabric. Pure wool upholstery can make skin feel itchy, and because wool is warming, it may be uncomfortable in certain settings. Wool may be blended with cotton or even cashmere to create a smoother fabric, increasing its versatility.

VELVET may be composed of a variety of fibers, including wool, silk, cotton, and synthetics. The allure of velvet is thanks to its thick, short pile on one side. It is soft and very durable, and can be used in almost any application.

Prints and patterns can be found in any of these fabrics, though they're most often associated with cotton; these designs offer both tactile and visual texture in a room. Prints may be mixed in with solids or combined with other patterns, as seen in fashion; in both realms, there must be a constant to unite different prints, whether it's color, scale, or theme. The print historically associated with France is *toile de Jouy*, which refers to pastoral or bourgeois scenes in a single color with a large repeat on white or natural color fabric. As with any classic motif, it has been tweaked and updated over the years to include different hues and unexpected scenes, but it remains quintessentially French.

1. VELVET

2. WOOL

3. PATTERNED LINEN

4. VELVET

5. VELVET

6. VELVET

7. LINEN

8. PATTERNED LINEN

9. LINEN

10. VELVET

11. PATTERNED COTTON

1

2

6

7

Give your windows a luxurious look with dramatic double-panel drapes. Consider extra length at the bottom, but bear in mind that six- to eight-inch puddles like these are best for drapes that stay open; opening and closing them will quickly dirty the bottoms.

FITTING PAINT FINISHES

IN FRENCH decorating, every surface—every wall, ceiling, and molding—is considered an opportunity to add texture. Interior paints come in a variety of finishes, from matte to high gloss, that can make subtle or bold contributions to the visual and tactile appeal of a room. To achieve your ideal texture on painted walls, ceilings, and woodwork, survey the options below. Keep in mind the conditions of the surfaces to be painted, the aesthetics of the room, and how much use the area gets—all factors in selecting the best finishes for your home.

FLAT PAINT has a matte finish that absorbs light. Because flat paint hides imperfections in the application of the paint and in the surface itself but is a bit tricky to wash, it is used most often on ceilings and sometimes on walls.

EGGSHELL PAINT is slightly more reflective than flat, and so it is easier to clean, making it a versatile choice for walls.

SATIN PAINT is similar to eggshell, though it has a bit more luster; it is easy to clean, so a good fit for walls in high-traffic areas and for molding and trim.

SEMIGLOSS PAINT is shiny and easy to wipe clean. It is a popular choice for window trim, doors, moldings, and walls and cabinetry in kitchens and bathrooms.

HIGH-GLOSS PAINT has a brilliant shine and saturated color and it stands up well to frequent cleaning. Because it will highlight imperfections, it is critical to carefully prepare the underlying base surface before painting. The reflective finish of high-gloss paint also makes small spaces appear larger.

LACQUER can be applied to new wood in order to create a mirrorlike shine. Because lacquers have limited applications and are hazardous to use and difficult to apply, consider an alternative, such as an ultra-high-gloss paint, to create the effect of lacquer on walls or woodwork.

Gilded frames, a brass kaleidoscope, and an eighteenth-century portrait of Louis XV's queen glow against a matte-black wall, creating a sultry mood in an interior hallway.

OPPOSITE Bold lacquered cornflower-blue walls make a traditional living room look fresh and daring. Oak and leather armchairs flank the mantel, which is adorned with an ostrich egg, a stone obelisk, and a lamp. The colors of the walls, upholstery, and rug might not be conventionally complementary, but in this daring arrangement, they create a beautiful and unique room. Its handsome but imposing furnishings look more approachable and modern thanks to the bright blue of the walls.

When refinishing an antique or vintage item, balance old and new. Bring the piece back to life with paint or upholstery, but let it show its age through imperfections, too.

ABOVE A blue-upholstered footstool set by a window gives the suggestion of activity and encourages a closer look at the view.

BELOW A 1790s Directoire beauty table with built-in mirror and candleholders is the perfect antique for the master bathroom; its time-worn metal elements emphasize its preciousness against the smooth marble tiles of the floor.

PRECEDING SPREAD, LEFT The living room's color palette is simple, but the textures are complex. The white sofa and chair are embellished by plush decorative pillows in luxe fabrics, a mohair blanket, and fringed trim. The fibrous sisal rug pleasantly contrasts with the sleek black lacquer coffee table.

PRECEDING SPREAD, RIGHT The compact but well-appointed bar is set with a silver cocktail shaker and ice bucket, amber cocktail glasses, and crystal decanters, all atop a neoclassical gilt console table. The surfaces and finishes on the console and drinkware are complemented by the polished tortoiseshell, the ceramic umbrella stand, and the Spanish-leather-and-silk-damask chair surrounding them. The original distressed leather of the chair back is accented by new silk damask and a fringed seat.

ABOVE Along a painted stone wall, natural fabric is used in an elegant way. A linen-topped side table supports a vintage-style lamp, fresh lavender from a local vendor, and a lantern found at a flea market.

BELOW In an ancient-looking wall nearly covered in ivy, a window peaks through and catches the sunlight. The sleek new window, the organic softness of the foliage, and the coarse stone provide a great example of layering textures as you might do on a sofa with linen, velvet, and cashmere.

OPPOSITE The door to the stone building is paneled wood with wrought-iron detail, under an iron-and-glass canopy reminiscent of Paris's famous Métro stations. The many materials combine to create rich texture and visual interest, even within the monochromatic color scheme.

PRECEDING SPREAD, RIGHT The many different materials used to build and maintain this centuries-old home make it a multilayered backdrop for decor.

ABOVE A gilt-bronze sconce with urn finials, bellflower swags, and fluted arms picks up the shimmer in the verdigris wall behind it; *verdigris* refers to the natural patina of copper.

BELOW A vintage table features a carved-wood base and an etched-glass top that's even more dazzling against the grainy hardwood floor.

OPPOSITE Above rough wide-plank floorboards, a gauzy white curtain billows over a stool perfectly placed for gazing out the kitchen window.

PRECEDING SPREAD, LEFT The vintage glass-and-Lucite desk is topped with an ostrich-skin table lamp by R+Y Augousti; tucked underneath is a glossy black shell stool, also by R+Y Augousti. The transparency of the desk allows it to overlap the silk-velvet curtains without looking crowded.

PRECEDING SPREAD, RIGHT This bedroom's stone walls and floors are softened by animal-hide rugs and plush linens on the hand-carved four-poster bed. These pieces loosen up the room and make it feel much warmer.

FRENCH FLOORS

In the composite that is French decorating, floors form the first layer of design. Floors are literally and figuratively the foundation of a room. There are many options for interior flooring, and each type has a variety of looks and finishes to choose from. So whether you're installing new floors in your home or refinishing the existing ones, you can give that first layer any look you like. Among the most common types of flooring in French decorating are hardwood, natural stone, and terra-cotta tile. Here are some notes to consider when mulling changes or updates to your floors:

HARDWOOD floors are very popular, and with good reason: they are available in a multitude of styles and finishes, and thanks to recent advances in sealants, they can be used throughout the house (traditional wisdom had been that wood was a poor choice in kitchens and baths, where water could cause the boards to warp and deteriorate; this is no longer a problem).

Wood floors are available in narrow strips of 2½ inches in width, or less, or in planks as wide as 8 inches. Wood strips may be arranged in parallel lines or in decorative parquets of varying intricacy, including the chevron or herringbone pattern very popular in France. Wide-plank wood floors tend to be associated with rustic settings, but as with other wood floors, their appearance can be transformed with stain, paint, or polish. Some species of wood, such as oak, are naturally harder than others; the harder the wood, the better the floors will hold up over time. But generally, good-quality wood floors with a durable finish are easy to care for with regular dusting and damp mopping. Every few years, wood floors can be refinished as needed depending on wear patterns, which allows you to maintain the look you've chosen or to try a new one—you can go from a light stain to a dark one to a painted floor.

TILE refers to any variety of clay baked into thin slabs. They may be glazed or unglazed ceramic, porcelain, or terra-cotta. Glazed tile has a thin coating of glass baked onto the ceramic, which protects the color and design of the tile and makes it easier to care for. Unglazed ceramic tile is known as quarry tile; it has a rougher surface than the glazed variety and is more porous. In order to keep quarry tile in good condition, it is best to have it sealed for protection from moisture and other stains. Porcelain tile may be glazed or unglazed; both varieties are very hard, nonporous, and resistant to signs of wear and tear. Because terra-cotta tiles are naturally porous and more vulnerable than other varieties, they require more maintenance, including sealing and regular waxing. If years of wear have dulled the appearance of the terra-cotta, the floors may be chemically stripped to bring back

the original color, then resealed. Tiles are traditionally used in kitchens and baths, but they can be beautiful in any room of a home—a bedroom or living room, for example—if you soften their look with area rugs.

STONE floors are prized for their natural beauty. The category includes very hard stones such as granite and marble and softer ones such as limestone, which is extremely popular in France. The softer a stone, the more susceptible it is to damage, but for many people, the appeal only increases due to the way natural stone evolves over time and the patina it develops. Hard and soft stones can be cleaned with dusting and mopping, though hard stones should still be sealed every few years, and soft stones may need a more intense cleaning every few years to refresh them. Stone floors look gorgeous in any area of a home, though stone can feel cold on bare feet in places like bathrooms, and special consideration should be given when using stone in work areas, such as the kitchen, where they may become wet and slippery, and where standing for long periods can be uncomfortable on such a hard surface.

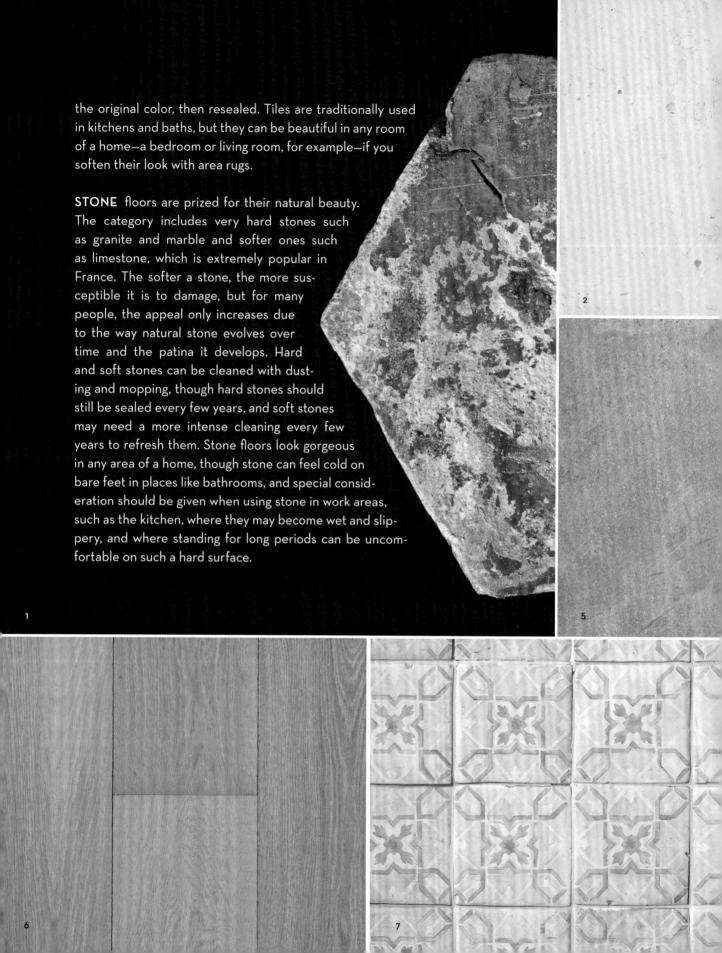

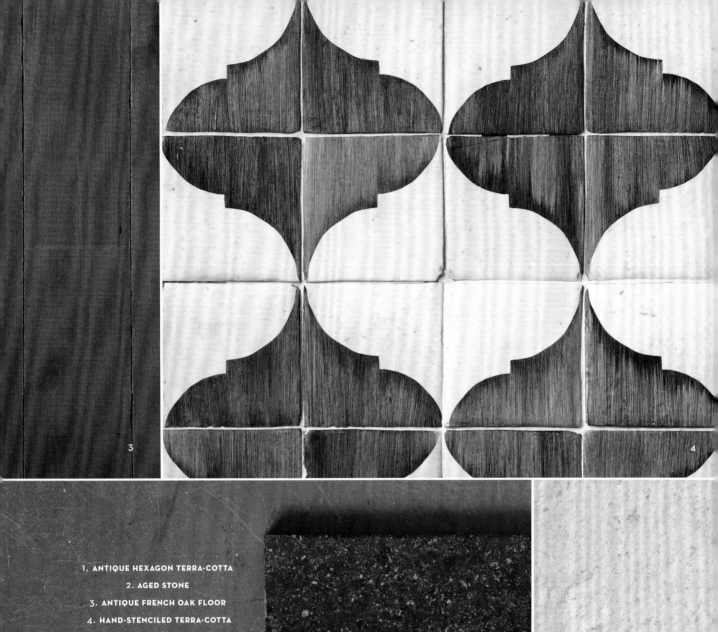

1. ANTIQUE HEXAGON TERRA-COTTA
2. AGED STONE
3. ANTIQUE FRENCH OAK FLOOR
4. HAND-STENCILED TERRA-COTTA
5. FRENCH LIMESTONE
6. MANOIR NAMUR WOOD
7. HAND-STENCILED TERRA-COTTA
8. FRENCH LIMESTONE
9. AGED LIMESTONE

1. BLACK CEMENT TILE
2. HAND-STENCILED MOORISH INSPIRED
3. MONTAIGNE CHARLEROI WOOD
4. TERRA-COTTA
5. CEMENT TILE MOORISH INSPIRED
6. HAND-STENCILED TERRA-COTTA
7. FRENCH LIMESTONE
8. STRAW TERRA-COTTA
9. WOOD INLAY

Consider floor-to-ceiling drapes to cover a doorway, and add sensuality and movement in the room. For a harmonious look, choose fabric in a similar shade to the walls.

JASON BASMAJIAN

When was your home built?

JB: Not sure of the exact date of the building but it is a Haussmann building.

What is its history?

JB: It was built as a residence located next to the famous Bon Marché.

When did it become yours?

JB: I have lived here for twelve years.

What drew you to your home? What do you love most about it?

JB: I loved the volume, light, and moldings. It was very classic but very modern at the same time. It immediately felt like home even though it was under renovation when I chose it.

How have you put your mark on it?

JB: I had the idea to keep the two major central rooms—the living and dining rooms—white and treated them as one space. I wanted the bedroom, kitchen, and foyer to be darker in tone and cozier. Lighting is important, so everything is on a dimmer, even in the bathrooms. The French electricians thought I was crazy.

Where do you look for decor inspiration?

JB: I look for inspiration when I travel, but I also find it in places least expected. Sometimes I come across interesting items, but overall I like keeping the space clean and clutter-free.

What are your favorite shops or sources for furnishings?

JB: I love Flair in Florence for furniture and objects. The owners, Franco Mariotti and Alessandra Tabacchi, are dear friends and have great taste. You can always find a perfect item. For more collectible important works of design, David Gill in London has the best pieces. For textiles, I love Dedar and Loro Piana Home.

Where do you find inspiration for interesting ways to use textiles?

JB: As artistic director for Brioni, I am inspired by luxury menswear fabrics—plaids, checks, stripes, flannel in wool, cashmere, linens. I love natural, elegant, noble fabrics.

Which pieces or rooms feature textures that you especially like?

JB: I like the leather in neutral tones on dining-room chairs. There are soft cashmere blankets everywhere, and in every room in both my Paris flat and my country house.

OPPOSITE Different shades of green are at play in one corner of the entry, from the olive-green paneled wall to a pillar candle, a potted plant, and a steel bench covered in moss-green bouclé fabric.

Other than textiles, what features of your home have appealing textures?

JB: I love my antique Moroccan rug in the living room. It makes it cozy to have friends here and sit on the floor around the coffee table and enjoy a casual evening. Otherwise I like the very formal table in the dining room in shades of grey, black, and taupe.

What is your favorite place to spend time in your home, and what do you do there?

JB: I love the living room for the wonderful light during the day and warm ambiance at night. On a warm, rainy summer night, it is magical to have all seven French windows open, candles lit, and enjoy a glass of wine while falling asleep on the sofa. I also love the kitchen for small dinners tête-à-tête. The dining room turns into a library if I stack art books and objects on the table. I like to keep moving things around but keep it clean. I work with a lot of patterns, colors, and textiles all day, so a soothing home is very welcome.

How would you describe the French approach to the details of a home?

JB: French lifestyle is all about elegance and style. It is a sort of unstudied chic that looks very put together. I think quality over quantity with furniture and objects, and there is a respect for mixing old and new. The French have a real savoir faire. Gracious entertaining is also a part of the French way of life. Time and care is put into a meal, from selecting recipes to buying the best-quality goods at the market, setting a table, and making your guest feel very at ease. I like my homes to be elegant but comfortable.

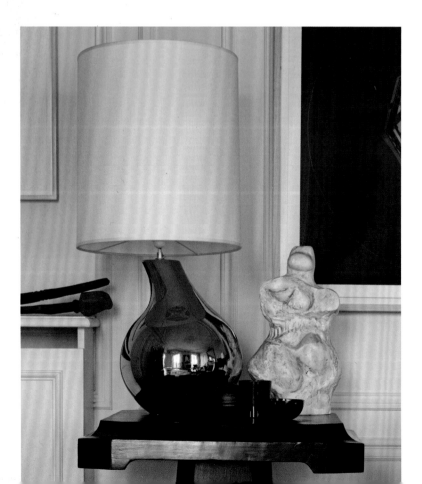

A silver lamp mimicking the organic form of a pear reflects the room, including a nineteenth-century plaster study for a sculpture and the 1940s mahogany side table below it. Their strikingly different forms create a curious arrangement.

OPPOSITE This bedroom has both soft and coarse elements, including plush blankets, velvet curtains, sisal carpeting, and 1940s wood benches covered in zebra skin.

Let animal hides show
their age. As with
leather, a bit of wear
only adds character
and interest.

HOME DESIGN CREDITS

This art-filled home was conceptualized and executed by award-winning designer Kristen McGinnis: 9, 25, 48 (top), 49, 81 (bottom)

Kristen McGinnis Design
kristenmcginnis.com
212-488-6820

Andrew Corrie and Harriet Maxwell Macdonald, the husband-and-wife team behind retailers Ochre and Canvas, have designed their home to reflect their unique aesthetic: 65, 113, 157, 174, 175, 188

Ochre
shop.ochrestore.com
212-414-4332
Canvas
shop.canvashomestore.com
212-461-1496

This interior was designed by its owner, Michael Bargo, for Michael Bargo Inc.: 93, 99, 103, 153, 192, 193

Michael Bargo Inc.
michaelbargo.com

These images depict the country home of Caroline Little: 6, 118, 119, 133, 156, 195, 196 (top, bottom), 199

The artistic director for Brioni, Jason Basmajian, decorated both his country and city homes: 12, 15, 17 (bottom), 20–21, 34–35, 53, 54, 61 (top), 94, 101, 108, 115, 119, 126, 129, 132, 144, 151, 168, 208, 210, 211

Jean-Louis Deniot is the homeowner, architect, and designer of this residence. He is the principal of the award-winning eponymous design firm: 2, 14, 18, 19, 30 (top), 46, 48 (bottom), 66, 67 (top), 69, 77, 79, 81 (top), 88 (bottom), 96, 98 (top), 109, 128 (top), 146, 155, 164, 167 (top, bottom), 172, 194 (top, bottom), 197

Jean-Louis Deniot
deniot.com
01 45 44 04 65

Josephine Rooney Duval is the architect and designer of these two homes: 134 (top, bottom), 135, 171

Josephine Rooney Duval
rooney-duval-architecture.com

New York–based architect and decorator Robert Couturier created this interior: 16, 31, 64, 107, 114, 148, 178, 179, 191

Robert Couturier
robertcouturier.com
212-463-7177

This home is the work of product and interior designer Liana Yaroslavsky: 56, 58, 67 (bottom), 102, 104–105, 170

This interior is the work of designer and antiques dealer Sidney Schatzky and Shelly Geffner: 17 (top), 100

This residence was designed by homeowner Lili Goldberg for herself and her husband, artist Jean-Claude Goldberg: 6, 30 (bottom), 57, 78, 122, 124, 125

Homeowner and designer Timothy Corrigan created this home: 5, 61 (bottom), 68, 157 (top)

timothy-corrigan.com
323-525-1802

Brigitte Langevin was the designer for the home where she resides with her husband, renowned photographer Marc Hispard: 26–27, 28, 80, 82, 85, 86, 110, 131

These photos were taken at the home of actress and singer Susan Malick: 33, 52, 62, 136, 200, 201 (bottom)

The home of Vincent Frey and his wife, Bianca, is built within the former archives of textile-design house Pierre Frey: 40, 42, 43 (top, bottom), 44, 45, 112 (top)

Pierre Frey
pierrefrey.com
212-421-0534

Alessandra Tabacchi and Franco Mariotti, owners of Flair Home Collection, designed this apartment: 55, 130, 173, 176, 198, 221

Flair Home Collection
flairhomecollection.com
212-274-1750

RESOURCES

Seek out these shops, showrooms, and websites to find the beautiful items seen in these pages and create a French-inspired interior of your own.

BUILDING AND RENOVATING

Benjamin Moore & Co.
855-724-6802
benjaminmoore.com

Boffi
31½ Greene Street
New York, NY 10013
212-431-8282
boffi.com

Dornbracht
800-774-1181
dornbracht.com

Enkeboll Designs
16506 Avalon Boulevard
Carson, CA 90746
866-578-2098
shopenkebolldesigns.com

Exquisite Surfaces
150 East 58th Street
Suite #9
New York, NY 10155
212-355-7990
xsurfaces.com

Fine Paints of Europe
800-332-1556
finepaintsofeurope.com

P. E. Guerin
23 Jane Street
New York, NY 10014
212-243-5270
peguerin.com

Ralph Lauren Paint
888-475-7674
ralphlaurenhome.com

Rioni Wood Products
4907 First Avenue
Brooklyn, NY 11232
718-499-4547
rioniwood.com

Sherle Wagner
300 East 62nd Street
New York, NY 10065
212-758-3300
sherlewagner.com

Stark Paint Colours
   by David Oliver
D&D Building
979 Third Avenue
10th Floor
New York, NY 10022
212-752-9000
starkpaint.com

Volevatch
108 rue du Cherche-Midi
75006 Paris
01 42 22 42 55
volevatch.fr

ART + ANTIQUES

Atelier Jean Torrens
   Antiquités SEMC
8 rue Lakanal
75015 Paris
01 48 28 47 08
antiques-jean-torrens.com

Au Débotté
19 rue Saint-Paul
75004 Paris
01 48 04 85 20

Aux Trois Singes
10 rue de Beaun
75007 Paris
33 6 75 55 44 57
aux3singes.com

Chahan Gallery
11 rue Lille
75007 Paris
01 47 03 47 00
chahan.com

Chelsea Gallery
533 Kings Road
London SW10 0TZ
020 7376 4000

1st Dibs
200 Lexington Avenue
10th Floor
New York, NY 10016
646-293-6693
1stdibs.com

Friedman Vallois
27 East 67th Street
New York, NY 10021
212-517-3820
vallois.com

Galerie Anne-Sophie
   Duval
Art Déco–XXème Siècle
5 quai Malaquais
75006 Paris
01 43 54 51 16
annesophieduval.com

Galerie Marc Philippe
4 rue de l'Université
75007 Paris
01 42 96 15 90
marcphilippe.fr

Galerie Sylvain Alban-
   Levy
33 quai Voltaire
01 42 61 25 42
Paris 75007
levyalban-antiques-paris
   .com

Geffner-Schatzky
   Antiques
40 Main Street
South Egremont, MA
   01258
413-528-0057
geffner-schatzky.com

Mantiques Modern
146 West 22nd Street, #1
New York, NY 10011
212-206-1494
mantiquesmodern.com

Peter Marigold
London
44 (0)208 880 06 90
petermarigold.com

James Sansum
33 East 68th Street
6th Floor
New York, NY 10065
212-288-9455
jamessansum.com

La Palférine
43 Avenue Bosquet
75007 Paris
01 45 56 93 81

L'Arc en Seine
31 rue de Seine
75006 Paris
01 43 29 11 02
arcenseine.com

Louis Bofferding
970 Lexington Avenue
New York, NY 10021
212-744-6725

Maison Gerard
53 East 10th Street, #A
New York, NY 10003
212-674-7611
maisongerard.com

Nicole Mugler
2 rue de l'Université
75007 Paris
01 42 96 36 45

Stéphane Olivier
10 rue Paul Bert
93400 Saint-Ouen
01 40 10 56 69
stephaneolivier.fr

Zerline
Marché Malassis
Central Patio
142 rue des Rosiers
93400 Saint-Ouen
6 98 27 04 40
zerline.com

OBJECTS, FURNITURE + HOME FURNISHINGS

Arne Jacobsen
FRITZ HANSEN
  HEADQUARTERS
Allerødvej 8
DK-3450 Allerød
Denmark
4817 2300
arne-jacobsen.com

Astier de Villatte
173 rue St.-Honoré
75001 Paris
01 42 60 74 13
astierdevillatte.com

Atelier Viollet
505 Driggs Avenue
Brooklyn, New York
  11211
718-782-1727
atelierviollet.com

Bergdorf Goodman
5th Avenue at 58th Street
New York, NY 10019
800-558-1855
bergdorfgoodman.com

Canvas
123 West 17th Street
New York, NY 10011
212-461-1496
canvashomestore.com

Caravane
6 rue Pavée
75004 Paris
01 44 61 04 20
caravane.fr

Cassina
155 East 56th Street
New York, NY 10022
212-245-2121
cassinausa.com

Chelsea Frames
197 Ninth Avenue
New York, NY 10011
212-807-8957
chelseaframes.com

Christian Liaigre
34 East 61st Street
New York, NY 10022
212-201-2338
christian-liaigre.fr

Christophe Delcourt
47 rue de Babylone
75007 Paris
01 42 71 34 84
christophedelcourt.com

Circa Lighting
405 Whitaker Street
Savannah, GA 31401
912-447-1008
circalighting.com

Cupboards and Roses
296 South Main Street
Route 7, PO Box 426
Sheffield, MA 01257
413-229-3070
cupboardsandroses.com

Design et Nature
5 rue d'Aboukir
75002 Paris
01 43 06 86 98

Deyrolle
46 rue du Bac
75007 Paris
01 42 22 30 07
deyrolle.fr

Elizabeth Bauer Design
43 Greenwich Avenue
New York, NY 10014
212-255-8625
elizabethbauerdesign.com

Evolution
120 Spring Street
New York, NY 10012
212-343-1114
theevolutionstore.com

Flair
88 Grand Street
New York, NY 10013
212-274-1750
flairhomecollection.com

Flamant Paris
8 place Furstemberg,
  8 rue de l'Abbaye
75006 Paris
01 56 81 12 40
flamant.com

Geneviève Prou
18 rue Duret
75116 Paris
01 45 00 22 40

Gilles Nouailhac
24 avenue de la Carelle
94290 Villeneuve-le-Roi
01 45 97 13 50
gillesnouailhac.com

Gracie
419 Lafayette Street, #5
New York, NY 10003
212-924-6816
graciestudio.com

Hermès
690 Madison Avenue
New York, NY 10065
212-308-3585
hermes.com

India Mahdavi
3 rue las Cases
75007 Paris
01 45 55 67 67
india-mahdavi.com

Jansen
905-563-1822
jansenfurniture.com

John Derian
6 East Second Street
New York, NY 10003
212-677-3917
johnderian.com

Koi Design
42 Southwood Park,
  Southwood Lawn Road
London N6 5SQ
01 208 340 4733
koidesign.co.uk

Modenature Paris
La Maison de Cedric
2 rue Camille Pelletan
13210 Saint-Rémy-de-
  Provence
4 32 60 12 83
modenature.com

Ochre
462 Broome Street
New York, NY 10013
212-414-4332
ochre.net

Oly
408 Greenwich Street
New York, NY 10013
212-219-8969
olystudio.com

Pierre Frey
979 Third Avenue
New York, NY 10022
212-421-0534
pierrefrey.com

Provence & Fils
20 bis rue François
  Chénieux
87000 Limoges
05 55 79 93 45
provence-et-fils.com

Ralph Vuolo Designs
Greenwich, CT
203-253-1414
New York, NY
212-369-0694
ralphvuolodesigns.com

Remains Lighting
130 West 28th Street
New York, NY 10001
212-675-8051
remains.com

Roche Bobois
200 Madison Avenue
New York, NY 10016
212-889-0700
roche-bobois.com

Ruzzetti and Gow
1015 Madison Avenue
New York, NY 10075
212-327-4281
ruzzettiandgow.com

R+Y Augousti
New York Design Center
200 Lexington Avenue,
　Suite 419
New York, NY 10016
646-293-6679
augousti.com

Steven Sclaroff
44 White Street
New York, NY 10013
212-691-7814
stevensclaroff.com

Susan Chalom
212-486-9207
susanchalom.com

Thomas Boog
52 rue de Bourgogne
75007 Paris
01 43 17 30 03
thomasboog.com

Treillage
418 East 75th Street
New York, NY 10021
212-535-2288
bunnywilliams.com/
　treillage

Van Baggum Collecties
　Recordweg 2
3821 AS Amersfoort
The Netherlands/Pays-Bas
0031(0)624532576
vanbaggumcollecties.com

Vitra
29 Ninth Avenue
New York, NY 10014
212-463-5750
vitra.com

WALLPAPERS + TEXTILES

Brunschwig & Fils
D&D Building
979 Third Avenue
12th Floor
New York, NY 10022
212-838-7878
brunschwig.com

Cowtan and Tout
979 Third Avenue
Suite 1022
New York, NY 10022
212-753-4488
cowtan.com

Farrow & Ball
D&D Building
979 Third Avenue
Suite 1519
New York, NY 10022
212-752-5544
us.farrow-ball.com

Georges Le Manach
　Claremont Inc.
Art and Design Building
1059 Third Avenue
2nd Floor
New York, NY 10065
212-486-1252
lemanach.fr

Jim Thompson America,
　Inc.
1694 Chantilly Drive
Atlanta, GA 30324
404-325-5004
jimthompson.com

Lelievre
13 rue du Mail
75002 Paris
01 43 16 88 00
lelievre.eu

Pierre Frey
D&D Building
979 Third Avenue
Suite 1611
New York, NY 10022
212-421-0534
pierrefrey.com

Rubelli
Donghia Showroom/
　D&D Building
979 Third Avenue
Suite 700
New York, NY 10022
212-935-3713
rubelli.com

Schumacher
D&D Building
979 Third Avenue
Suite 832
New York, NY 10022
212-415-3900
fschumacher.com

Stark Wallcovering
D&D Building
979 Third Avenue
10th Floor
New York, NY 10022
212-752-9000
starkcarpet.com

Zuber
200 East 59th Street
New York, NY 10022
212-486-9226
zuber.fr

GLOSSARY

ANTIQUE: a work of art, piece of furniture, or decorative object that existed at and is in the style of an earlier time. U.S. Customs defines a work of art and a piece of furniture as antique if it dates to before 1840.

ART DECO: a decorative style prevalent between the first and second world wars. The style is known for its use of geometric shapes, sharp angles, strong colors, and ornamentation. Art deco is epitomized by the works exhibited at the 1925 Exposition Internationale des Arts Décoratifs et Industriels Modernes (International Exhibition of Modern and Industrial Decorative Arts) in Paris.

ART GLASS: known for its expressive use of color, pattern, and texture in a variety of handmade objects, including but not limited to vases, bowls, and paperweights. Due to the work of Emile Gallé, Daum Frères, and René Lalique, French art glass is typically associated with the art nouveau period.

ART NOUVEAU: stimulated by the disorderliness of the natural world, the "new art" developed between the 1880s and World War I. Particularly associated with France, the art nouveau style was also referred to as style Jules Verne and le style Métro, and features stylized natural and botanical motifs.

BAROQUE: the baroque period in architecture, painting, and sculpture spanned the seventeenth and eighteenth centuries. It is particularly distinguished by its strong sensuousness and high expression of drama, movement, and tension. Additionally, the furniture and decoration of the Louis XIV period is labeled baroque.

BATTEN-AND-BOARD: a siding that alternates wide boards and narrow battens that can be applied to either the interior or exterior of a house.

BOISERIE: the carved woodwork and paneling prevalent in seventeenth- and eighteenth-century French interiors that can often be seen in gilt. Boasting both decorative and practical purposes, boiserie contributes to not only the decor but also to the insulation of a room.

BRIC-A-BRAC: miscellaneous collections of small decorative objects or ornaments displayed within a house. A term used often during the Victorian era.

BROCANTE: the French term for a secondhand trade and flea market.

CHEVRON: in ornament, a zigzag design that can be seen on wooden flooring or molding. Similar to herringbone, the chevron pattern is distinguished by wooden pieces with diagonal edges that meet to form a repeating V.

CHINOISERIE: popular in the Louis XV period in France, chinoiserie depicts whimsical Chinese-like decorative motifs that are Western interpretations of Oriental designs copied from Chinese imports.

CLASSICAL: the term *classical* refers to the artistic, literary, architectural, and sculptural ideals of the ancient Greeks and Romans. For something to be labeled classical, it must have either an antique source or be part of an established degree of excellence.

COMMODE: typically understood as a chest of drawers or a cabinet that is low in stature. Throughout the history of France, there existed various interpretations of the commode. During the Louis XIV period, *bureau commode* was used to describe a large table with drawers. During the Regency and Louis XV periods, a commode was generally *bombé*, or outwardly curving, in shape and understood as the most typical piece of furniture at that time. Additionally, *commode* can refer to a nightstand, bedside cabinet, or chest, and can be a term used for *toilet*.

CONSIGNMENT: a means to buy and sell products in which goods are delivered to a store or market under the agreement that payment for the goods will be made once and only if the goods are sold.

CONSOLE TABLE: originally popular in eighteenth-century France and England, a shelflike two-legged table attached to a wall. Also known as a *pier table*.

CORBEL: made of materials such as wood, plaster, and marble, an architectural bracket that extends from the surface of the wall and supports or appears to support a ceiling beam or other horizontal members.

CUBISM: the forerunner for abstract art, invented by Pablo Picasso and Georges Braque in 1907–1909, it rejects a realistic depiction of its subject in favor of a more expressive depiction. The cubist artist strove to capture the essence of his subject through the use of abstracted shapes and planes. Influenced by the cubist artists, French designers adopted the cubist aesthetic and worked it into their interior decoration.

DADO: the lower part of a wall below the chair rail.

DIRECTOIRE: the Directoire style lasted from 1795 to 1799 during the Directory in France. The Directoire style is known not only for its transition toward a closer imitation of the antique but also for its use of Revolutionary emblems.

EGGSHELL: similar to an egg, *eggshell* refers to a painted finish with a soft, dull, low luster.

EMPIRE: lasting roughly from 1804 to 1820, the Empire period marked the emergence of the neoclassical style in architecture, art, and decoration, combined with a great interest in Egyptian and other ancient motifs.

ENGAGED COLUMNS: attached to the wall, an engaged column shows its roundness while being structural and/or decorative.

ENTABULATURE: in classical architecture, it is the crowning feature of molding that consists of the architrave, frieze, and cornice and rests on the capital.

FRENCH WINDOWS: both functional and decorative, this double-leafed, multipaned doorlike window extends down to the floor and enables people to enter and leave a room. Sometimes referred to as French doors, French windows allow more natural light into a house as well as divide a room while still maintaining its openness of space. They are a great way to let the outdoors in and vice versa.

FRIEZE: the central portion of the entablature located above the architrave and below the cornice, it could be embellished with decorative sculpture or carving. In furniture, the frieze is the underframing of a table between the top surface and the legs.

GARGOYLE: the term is from the Old French for *throat*. It is a creature that serves as a rainspout in Gothic architecture and is decoratively placed along the top of a parapet or roof. In folklore, the gargoyle has become known as a protective spirit.

GARNITURE: any motif used to adorn, enhance, and embellish a surface or area.

GILT: to be covered thinly with gold leaf or gold dust.

GOTHIC: the Gothic period is also known as the Middle Ages and it is the period that lasted approximately from 1150 to 1500 in Europe. Gothic architecture peaked in France in the middle of the twelfth century. It is the only European architectural style not based on classical forms. One recognizes Gothic architecture by the use of elements such as the pointed arch, ribbed vault, and flying buttresses.

HERRINGBONE: seen in woodwork, brickwork, and stonework, a geometric mosaic created by two or more bands of material laid side by side. Similar to chevron, the material is laid at angles, so that the alternate courses point in opposite directions.

HIGH GLOSS: a paint's sheen or shine or a wood-furniture finishing process that results in an external surface with a high sheen or shine. High-gloss paint is typically more durable than flatter paint, which is more porous and therefore more difficult to clean.

KILIM: a pileless, flat-woven, reversible, often patterned, handwoven rug or other covering made in various parts of the Middle East, eastern Europe, and Turkestan.

LACQUER: a colored or opaque varnish made of shellac dissolved in alcohol, sometimes with pigment added, that dries to form a hard protective coating for wood, metal, and other surfaces.

LANCET ARCH: taking its name from being shaped like the tip of a lance, the narrow pointed arch is a feature of early Gothic architecture and furniture.

LINTEL: a horizontal piece of wood or stone that spans over a door, window, or other opening to help carry the weight of the structure above it.

LOUIS XIII: the reign of Louis XIII fell within the French late Renaissance period, which lasted from 1589 to 1643. The Italian Renaissance remained the dominant influence during this period on both architecture and interior decoration alongside Dutch and Flemish influences. More specifically, wall paneling became much more important within interiors at this time.

LOUIS XIV: Louis XIV, France's Sun King, ruled from 1643 to 1715, and his reign is directly associated with the baroque style, which created rooms and furniture that were giant in scale and adorned with rich decorations and strong colors.

MALACHITE: a sea-green to dark-green stone that is used for making ornamental articles and was used for amulets in ancient Egypt.

MANSARD ROOF: the mansard roof is named after the late French Renaissance architect François Mansart, who frequently used this type of roof. It is a hipped roof that has two slopes on each side. The lower portion is very steep and the upper portion is less extreme. The mansard roof allows for a useful interior space.

MANTEL: part of the chimneypiece, a shelf that projects above the fireplace.

MANTELPIECE: the decorative border around a fireplace.

MANTELSHELF: a horizontal shelf above the fireplace.

MARCHÉ: a French market.

MARQUETRY: popular in the Renaissance period and also in eighteenth-century France and England, a decorative work in which complex patterns are created through setting different pieces of material, such as colored woods, tortoiseshell, and horn, into veneered surfaces. Marquetry is found in furniture and in various wooden decorative accessories.

MATTE: the opposite of high gloss, a dull finish with no real sheen. Rather then reflect light, a matte finish absorbs light.

MEDALLION: a decorative ceiling accent, often cast in plaster, from the center of which light fixtures are often hung.

MEDIEVAL: (See Gothic.)

MILLINERY: the business or work of designing, making, trimming, or selling women's hats.

MODERN: the architecture, furniture, and furnishings of today, at times marked by a conscious break with the past. The modern style is recognized for its functional quality and lack of ornamentation, as well as its constantly changing style due to the multitude of influences in today's society.

NEOCLASSIC: a movement that originated in Rome in the mid-eighteenth century marked by the revival of the classical as a reaction against the excesses of the baroque and rococo styles and as an effect of the discoveries at Herculaneum and Pompeii. The Louis XVI style is known to have greatly embraced the neoclassical.

OBELISK: an upright four-sided decorative object that is square or rectangular at its base and gradually tapers as it rises and ends in a pyramid-shaped top.

PANEL: typically a flat surface enclosed by a frame, at times decorated with moldings, carvings, paintings, applied fabrics, and wallpapers. In window treatments, a square or rectangular piece of fabric with finished edges that falls from the top of the window to the bottom or to the floor.

PATINA: a film or coloration, often considered attractive, that develops on a number of surfaces, including stone, metal, wood, and others, over time.

PUDDLE: found in formal drapery treatments, a small pool of excess fabric that collects on the floor below drapes.

QUATREFOIL: the Gothic symbol for the cross and the four Evangelists. An ornamental stylized four-leaf clover often seen in Gothic decorations, such as window tracery, interior carved-wood decoration, and furniture.

RÉGENCE: the Regency period is a transitional time that lasted from 1700 to 1730, connecting the Louis XIV baroque period with the Louis XV rococo period.

RENAISSANCE: the transitional movement from about the fourteenth century to about the end of the seventeenth century in which Europe saw a rebirth and revival of art, architecture, philosophy, and literature based on classic Greek and Roman models.

ROCOCO: the rococo period lasted from 1730 to 1760 and is most specifically applied to the Louis XV period. The delicate intricacies and curvatures of the furniture created during the Régence period was further developed in the rococo period. Painted decorations and ornate high-relief carvings prospered using twirling leaves, asymmetrical C- and S-shaped scrolls, flowers, and fantastic whorls.

ROSETTE: a popular motif since the Gothic ages, *rosette* is French for little roses. A rosette is a rose-shaped decoration that is typically a circle with petals growing out from a central point.

SCANDINAVIAN MODERN: emerging at the same time as modernism, in the 1930s, it is a simple, refined version of the Empire style that combines modernism with the the unique characteristics of Scandinavia, such as the focus on natural beauty. Decorative elements are sparse, and walnut and teak are the woods most often used.

SECOND EMPIRE: the period in France that lasted approximately from 1852 to 1871 and is marked by the development of a heavily ornate style of furniture, architecture, and decoration, which combined Empire with Louis XV fashions.

SECRÉTAIRE: French for "desk."

SETTEE: a long, soft seat with arms and a carved or upholstered back originally designed for two or more persons. The settee is an alteration of the Gothic piece, the settle, which was a bench with back and arms.

TAXIDERMY: the art and practice of preparing and preserving animal skins, as well as stuffing and mounting them into lifelike forms.

TIEBACK: a strip or device used to pull a curtain to the side of a window, creating an ornamental swelling of fabric that appears above the tieback.

TRANSOM: the upper part of a window or a small window that fits over the top of a door, a transom is primarily decorative in that it enables additional light to enter the room; it is also used for cross-ventilation.

TRESTLE TABLE: also referred to as the sawbuck table, this seventeenth-century tabletop is supported by X-shaped trestles or two-legged standards.

TROMPE L'OEIL: meaning "fools the eye," trompe l'oeil is the detailed style that uses pictorial elements such as perspective, foreshortening, and shadows to make a work appear three-dimensional. The technique requires an artist to have a great understanding of the nuances of light and its effect on color.

TUFTED: an upholstery technique where the covering fabric and the padding are tied back in a pattern, creating little "pillows" between the depressions usually secured with a knot or button. Reaching its popularity during the Victorian period, in which it was fashionable for furniture to appear overstuffed, tufting enabled the fabric to conform to the curves of the unit. Headboards, ottomans, and sofas are examples of furniture upholstered this way, a technique often used on leather.

VENEER: thin slices of material, usually of wood, that are both protective and ornamental and that can be arranged on both furniture and walls in various ways. Veneers are placed on top of an inferior wood, so that the area appears to have been constructed with a finely grained, beautifully colored wood.

WROUGHT IRON: a tough and malleable form of iron that is easily forged and welded.

ACKNOWLEDGMENTS

This book could not have been completed without the help of some very important and special people. First and foremost, to the generous homeowners and incredibly fabulous designers and architects who opened their homes and projects for this book: Michael Bargo, Jason Basmajian, Andrew Corrie, Timothy Corrigan, Robert Couturier, Jean-Louis Deniot, Josephine Duval, Bianca Frey, Vincent Frey, Shelly Geffner, Lili and Jean-Claude Goldberg, Nathaniel Goldberg, Marc Hispard, Brigitte Langevin, Caroline Little, Harriet Maxwell MacDonald, Susan Malick, Alessandra and Franco Mariotti, Kristen McGinnis, Sidney Schatzky, Natalie Sutton, and Liana Yaroslavsky. I hope this book captures the beauty of your homes and projects.

To the wonderful Aussie photographer Jonny Valiant (and his wonderful team of Zach Callahan and Alberto Arias). Your ability to use natural light captured the essence and purity of the homes and projects. I never imagined that the photographs could be as beautiful as the spaces themselves.

To my writer, Brenna McLoughlin. Your eloquent words and phrases truly captured my vision for this book. Just as important, you reminded me that you cannot force creativity, and your warm smile and energy provided much-needed passion to get this project over the finish line.

To Mary Spencer Morten, Maggie McVeigh, and Eliza Crater. Mary and Maggie, you kept me organized and efficient when I was traveling back and forth to France and throughout the entire project. Eliza, your daily assistance kept the book moving forward. I truly cannot thank each of you enough.

To all of my colleagues and friends, especially Susan Becher (and her fabulous team), Brenna Goldberg, Elizabeth Blitzer, Ann Feldstein, Jaime Jimenez, Christiane Lemieux, Jon Morato, George Nunno, Lauren Paul, Molly Peterson, Katharina Plath, Emily Reaman, Lyn Schroeder, and Katie Woolsey. You gave me access to many of the homes in this book, and your friendship and support really made this book possible.

To the best studio mates in New York City: Vico Zabel, Van Peele, and the ringmaster, David Lewis Taylor. I am sure that if you had to hear one more thing about this book you were going to send me back to France for good. David, you're my mentor, my cheering squad, and a dear friend; I could not have done this without you.

Thanks to the Clarkson Potter team that made this all possible, especially my editor, Aliza Fogelson. You approached me with the general idea of creating a lavishly illustrated and informational book, and then let me run wild. You focused my vision without jeopardizing the artistic integrity of the book, and for that I am most appreciative.

To my family: Mom, Dad, Megan, and Harley. Your love and support kept me sane throughout this entire process. You inspire me every day and I love you.

Finally, to Ryan Welsh, who not only served as my wave of acceptance but also supported and loved me through the craziest of times. You've guided me through the process, never accepting less than my best, and always reminded me that creativity makes me happy.

INDEX